D1147251

Derbyshire Traditions

80p

Derbyshire Traditions

by

Clarence Daniel

Dalesman Books
1975

The Dalesman Publishing Company Ltd.,
Clapham (via Lancaster), North Yorkshire
First published 1975
© Clarence Daniel 1975

ISBN: 0 85206 285 0

Printed and Bound in Great Britain by
Ellesmere Press Ltd, Mill Lane, Skipton, North Yorkshire

Contents

The cover illustrations depict the legend of the severed hand (see chapter 4). The front cover painting by Bruce Danz shows Sir Hugo de Burdett slaying his wife Lady Johanne. The back cover sketch is of ancient carved heads said to represent characters in the legend —a third head is now missing.

Line drawings are by the author. Photographs on pages 34 (top), 36, 54 and 56 are by E. Hector Kyme, and on pages 34 (bottom), 35, 53 (top) and 55 by W. H. Brighouse.

Bakewell, a centre of witchcraft in the early seventeenth century (chapter 7)

Introduction

THIS book is an attempt to get away from the beaten paths of Derbyshire topography and discover some nooks and crannies of history and tradition which still remain unexplored, or which have only been partially investigated. All too often, when we pick up a book on the county, we are shepherded along familiar routes to familiar places to read familiar stories. So many authors appear to write as though their readers have only just discovered Derbyshire and consequently their books have little that is new to offer; at least not to the serious student and the seasoned enquirer.

And so, while I fully appreciate and endorse Byron's comment that "there are things in Derbyshire as noble as in Greece or Switzerland," I have not set out to conduct a Grand Tour by following the pilgrim way to Buxton, Dovedale, the Matlocks, Chatsworth, Haddon, Hardwick, Kedleston, Eyam, Castleton and other places which so often seem to be regarded as the sum total of Derbyshire's interest and appeal. Any allusion in the following pages to the stately homes is purely incidental, and the reader may have no fear of an attack of claustrophobia by the exploration of show caverns whose stalactitic and stalagmitic beauties have been so often and so faithfully described. Neither has any attempt been made to impose a further strain on superlatives with which to portray the scenic charms of Monsal Dale, Dovedale, the Hope Valley and Kinderscout. Nor have I ventured to describe examples of ecclesiastical architecture which have already been dealt with by experts in this field. No, this book is more a ramble into the fields of folk-lore; an effort to rediscover some of the fancies and fantasies of our forefathers, although much of the material is basically historical in character. And I hope that those who join me in this fairy-tale journey will reach the same conclusion as John Ruskin when he wrote:- "Derbyshire is a lovely child's alphabet; an alluring first lesson in all that is admirable; and powerful chiefly in the way it engages and fixes attention."

By way of postscript, attention may be drawn to physical changes which have recently taken place and which have some bearing on two of the chapters in this book. The female statue on the lower side of Chatsworth bridge, which was victim of an accident when it fell from the pier, has unfortunately been replaced with a masculine figure which rather spoils the effect of the story. The Warren Stone has also been exposed to full view by reconstruction work on the A6 which has involved a re-contouring of the river banks so that it now stands in naked isolation in the middle of a much wider stream.

1. The Drama of Demon's Dale

POETRY is a pied piper whose music sometimes lures its reader into the half-light of a land of legend. Many an old verbal tradition has been preserved by minstrels who have enshrined its theme in ballad form, and it has lived on in an enchanted castle of verse designed by some forgotten architect in words. The lyrics of these ancient folk songs have survived, while their accompanying melodies have long since been forgotten. Such is the story of Hulac Warren and Hedessa; a story which has something of the charm and colour, the romance and mystery of Greek mythology. Yet it is a sinister story of some ancient attempt at abduction and rape which may have been adopted as a pagan morality myth to warn men of the perils of unrestrained passion.

The story may have been known to the men who built and occupied the prehistoric fortress on the brow of Great Finn which overlooks the site where the incident happened. Standing within the mounds of this ancient defensive settlement, with slopes of grass and treacherous limestone screes falling dizzily away to the river Wye as it writhes through the valley far below, one gathers the impression that these ancient hunters and warriors not only had an instinct for secure military strategy, but an eye for beauty as they looked across a landscape of limestone crags, dense woods, tumbling streams and waves of hills that recede into the distance until they wash against the far horizon, They must often have felt the freezing fingers of wintry gales on their rugged faces, but they knew also the soft caress of flower-scented zephyrs in summer . . .

A landmark in the legend is the Warren Stone; a weathered crag of limestone lying in the elbow of a bend in the river Wye not far from Ashford-in-the-Water. Washed on every side by the waters of the river, it could almost be mistaken for the broken pier of a former bridge. Tradition says that Hulac Warren, leader of a race of giants who lived in the gloomy recesses of nearby Demon's Dale, was here turned into stone as punishment for attempting to defile Hedessa, a beautiful shepherdess whom he waylaid and carried to his lair.

Demon's Dale was referred to by a 15th century writer, William Worcester, in his *Itinerarum*:—"The Wye runs by the town of Marnsdale (Monsal Dale), a valley called Dymynsdale, where spirits are tortured, which is a marvellous entrance into the land of Peke, where souls are tormented . . . ." The same sinister place is recalled in an old jingle which mentions several local landmarks:-

The Old Woman of Demon's Dale,
The Pipes of Shacklow,
The Fiddler of Finn,
Gather them all in.

The story has been preserved by John Howe, a poet by calling and tallow chandler by trade, who was born in 1777 at Litton Slack, near Cressbrook, and whose only education was afforded by a night-school. Encouraged in his cultural tastes by Madam Eliza Dorothy Blore, he published his *Trifles Light as Air* in 1816. In a poem on Monsal Dale he tells at length the story of Hedessa, and how much is fact and how much fantasy has to be judged by the reader. Here are a few lines from the poem:

Beneath the Hough where transverse valleys meet,
Is Demon's Dale, a dreary lone retreat—
Need I relate (what neighbouring peasants say),
How Hulac Warren here concealed lay,
Surprised and carried to his horrid den,
The fairest daughter of the sons of men;
An humble shepherdess . . .
Chance led Hedessa through the verdant grove,
To spend the evening in the cool alcove,
Whence from thicket springing on his prize,
His yell triumphant rumbles through the skies;
Dread imprecations through each cavern roars,
She from the Fates and Gods relief implores,
With grief o'erpowered she instantly expires—
The tears dissolved beneath the hill retires—
Hence rose the Hedess Spring.
Hulac blasphemed the Gods and to atone
The heinous crime was turned to Warren Stone.

Another writer, a former local magistrate, gave a slightly different prose version of the story and refers to the villain of the piece as Hector Warren. He tells how the captured Hedessa pleaded a settled love, having pledged her affections elsewhere, and steadfastly resisted Warren's amorous advances, whereupon—"Enraged by her unflinching fidelity, Hector attempted to secure her by force. He seized the gentle form, and stifling her cries, carried her to the peak of yon cavernous tors. Standing on that overhanging ledge, where the

The Warren Stone, a weathered crag of limestone associated with the drama of Demon's Dale.

honey-flower and wild rose twine in undisturbed possession, the frenzy of despair came to the soul of Hedessa. A power superhuman was bestowed upon her by the gods, and with one desperate bound she freed herself from the arm that encircled her, but oh! sad to tell, her life was the penalty of the struggle, for she fell from the fearful height. Fragments of the rock from which Hedessa fell, form the circle round the spot in which the body lies, securing the enclosure (now sacred ground) from the intrusion of whatever is impure. Near the place where my loved one fell, a stream of pure water, pure as her own soul, gushed forth into being; and while these mountains, and these woods and valleys remain, the spirit of my Hedessa will visit these scenes, and bless with its presence the flowing water of the Hedess spring . . ."

And so the waters of the Hedess Spring bubble out of the limestone rocks, eternally weeping sad, symbolic tears in mourning for the lovely shepherdess. And so, too, waist deep in the chilly waters, the petrified giant pays his eternal penance as the river seeks to cleanse him from his awful guilt. And pedestrians in former days, walking between Ashford and Taddington, used to edge furtively away to the other side of the road, fearful of the haunted spot which still reminds us of the long past drama of Demon's Dale.

11

2.

The Mermaid's Pool

Woman and fish, so strangely blent in one,
So fables tell, and so old legends run.
Now on the wave greeting the new-born day;
Now on the velvet bank in sportive play;
And when prevailed the part of woman fair,
Into long locks it curled its golden hair,
Breathes the soft zephyrs as they gently rise,
And its fair bosom heaves with human sighs;
But when the fish prevails beneath the tides,
Like lightning it a scaly monster glides;
And in its watery cavern must remain
Till Easter Sunday morning comes again.

By the flick of a finger we turn from a page dealing with an ancient allegory set in the pastoral scenes around Monsal Dale, to one dealing with a landscape that is grim and austere, and yet one which possesses its own awe-inspiring grandeur — Kinder Scout. In summer, when the stretches of marsh and moorland are flecked with tufts of silky white cotton-grass fluttering in the breeze; or autumn when the heather smoulders like a mauve fire among green islands of bilberry and clusterberry briars, Kinder Scout reigns in smiling majesty over a primitive kingdom of heath and bracken, escarpment and crag, cascading water and still pools. But in winter, when treacherous mists swirl and eddy like currents in a vapour sea, and the landscape is bleached and drained of colour, or frozen into a silent sea of snow and ice, Kinder then assumes the character of a tyrant enthroned in a kingdom of sinister shadow and lurking fear. Then the scene becomes utterly changed to one patterned with nightmare shapes, and influenced by relentless and fierce forces, savage silences and sullen moods.

Marked on a large-scale map showing the Kinder Scout region you will find a small area of water called the Mermaid's Pool, and legend claims that this tiny lake or tarn has some mysterious and mystical relationship with the far-off Atlantic Ocean, and that its waters are salt and bitter to the taste. No animal will pause to drink its brackish water; no fish can survive within its gloomy depths; no wild fowl fly over its surface or build their nests among the reeds which grow at its margin! The place has an atmosphere of melancholy; a sense of desolation which suggests that some malign influence has cast a spell over the place. Indeed, it might be described as the Dead Sea of Derbyshire.

There is no doubt a perfectly simple and rational explanation to account for the brackishness of the water. Perhaps it is tainted by the peat and decayed moorland vegetation. But what induces the feeling of gloom and eeriness? Is it haunted? Or is it a place of evil enchantment? Tradition insists that it is both, for the Pool is reputed to be the haunt and home of a mermaid who becomes visible to human eyes on Easter Eve, and that those who see her bathing in the magic pool will become endowed with immortality, or otherwise will be lured to their death.

Mrs. Humphry Ward has woven the legend into the story told in her novel *David Grieve*, and J. B. Firth in his *Highways and Byways of Derbyshire* says: "Opinions may differ very much as to the merits of the opening chapters, and the skill with which the indefinable atmosphere of the moors is transferred to the pages of her book. In this respect Mrs. Ward has done for Kinderscout what the Brontes did for the Haworth and Keighley moors, and those who have time to spare will find reward in exploring for themselves the course of the Kinder, the little Red Brook where David set his miniature water-wheels, the ruined smithy where he sailed his boats in an iron pan, the sheds at Clough End where he listened to the preacher, the mountain torrent of the Downfall where Kinder comes roaring down in flood time through a steep, stony ravine, and the Mermaid's Pool where Jenny Crum was drowned, and to which the two children paid their midnight visit on Easter Eve . . ."

A regular visitor to the Pool on Easter Eve was a retired soldier named Aaron Ashton, of Hayfield, who coveted the legendary gift of immortality. When he was a child, Aaron was taken by his parents to Manchester in 1745 to see the rebels, and upon reaching manhood he enlisted in the Army and was a casualty at Bunker's Hill, being wounded by the same shot that killed another Derbyshire soldier, Major Shuttleworth, of Hathersage. Although his pilgrimages were never rewarded by a glimpse of the mermaid, Aaron lived on until the patriarchal age of 104, dying in the year 1835. Perhaps the mythical mermaid exerted some charm of longevity as a reward for his patience, perseverance and loyalty!

The mistress of this tiny inland sea had a talented minstrel in Henry Kirke who wrote a ballad telling of an infatuated shepherd lad who spurned the affections of mountain maids in favour of the mermaid's bewitching charms. He represented the mermaid as a siren who cheated men of the promise of immortality and lured them to destruction by her beauty of form and voice!

There is a land within a northern clime
Where many a mountain reaches to the clouds,
That rest their billowy fleeces on its head,
And roll adown its rugged, storm-rent sides.
At foot of such a mountain in this land
There lies a pool, dark and mysterious,
Shadowed by blackened rocks, and sedges drear,
In which no reedy warbler builds its nest;
No heather nods its bells unmusical
Around its banks, no sombre-coated bee
Hums over it a busy melody;
No speckled trout or dark-backed umber there
Wake the still waters with their circling leaps;
No chattering grouse drops in the doubtful wave
Feathers that float like tiny argosies;
Nor furry-footed coney stops to drink
Its waters salt as those their watch that keep
Over the doomed towns of Palestine.
With solemn awe the lonely shepherd treads
Past the weird margin of the mountain tarn,
Fearing the sprite that dwells within its depths,
And rot, and ague, and a thousand ills
He thinks such fearsome folks are wont to give
To those that trespass on their sovereignty.

But one there was a sprightly lad and tall,
And gifted with a face in which for mastery
Action and thought seemed always combating,
Who always felt attracted to the pool,
And sat for many hours plumbing its depth
With anxious eyes; but nought saw he therein
Save the reflection of his comely face.
Warning he had full oft from wiser men
To meddle not in such a dangerous quest,
Nor seek for death where death was surely found:
For 'tis believed that on a certain eve
When summer fruits are ripe, and in the sky
The stars can scarcely light their shining lamps,
And the soft air is strangely musical
With the faint hum of fairy merriment,
A maiden, strangely fair, but strangely formed,
Rises from out the pool, and by her songs
And heavenly beauty lures to shameful death
The luckless wight who hears her melodies.

But youth is curious, and the shepherd lad
Longed with intense desire to see the maid.
He dreamt of her by night, her white arm seemed
To lock him in a clinging, fond embrace;
She haunted him by day as moodily
He watched beside the pool, and seemed to see
In each reflected cloud her drapery.

At last the night arrived, the sun just dipped
His rosy fingers in the pathless sea,
Leaving the world not dark, but hardly light;
The waning stars scarce marked the azure sky,
And zephyrs gently cooled the heated earth:
'Twas just the hour when night and morning meet
When, watching still, the boy sat eagerly,
On a huge stone that darkened all the pool;
When suddenly the wave gleamed fitfully
With sudden light, as in the tropic seas
The lambent waves shine with phosphoric glare,
And brighter grew the water, and the air
Was filled with music ravishingly sweet.

The youth stood gazing at these mysteries,
And saw from out the troubled waves arise
A maiden, clothed alone in loveliness;
Her golden hair fell o'er her shoulders white,
And curled in amorous ringlets round her breasts;
Her eyes were melting into love, her lips
Had made the very roses envious;
Withal a voice so full, and yet so clear,
So tender, made for loving dialogues.
And then she sang—sang of undying love
That waited them within her coral groves
Beneath the deep blue sea, and all the bliss
That mortals made immortal could enjoy,
Who lived with her in sweet community.

She sang, and stretching out her rounded arms,
She bade him leap and take her for his own—
With one wild cry he leapt, and with a splash
That roused the timid moorhen from her nest,
Sank 'neath the darkling wave for evermore.

A similar story to the above is told of the Black Meer of Morridge
—a stretch of water on the bleak moors between Buxton and Leek.
Indeed the two stories are so alike that one suspects some chronicler
may have been infringing copyright! The Black Meer was claimed

to be bottomless; cattle refused to drink its waters; fish could not survive in its brackish depths, and birds never flew over it. Moreover, it was haunted by a mermaid who had the same personal magnetism for males, and who rose from its depths at midnight. The legend is kept alive by the name of a nearby inn—the Mermaid Inn.

One night, many years ago, a mermaid **was** seen there and rescued from a most distressing situation. Had it not been for the legend of the mermaid, murder would surely have been committed at this lonely spot. A number of men were gathered at the Cock Inn one wild and wintry night when the conversation veered to the sinister stories concerning the haunted meer; stories which made it avoided by timid and superstitious folk. One member of the company stoutly averred his willingness, for the consideration of five shillings, to visit the haunted tarn that same midnight. His comrades accepted the challenge and subscribed between them the necessary money, stipulating that the man must leave his stick at the brink of the pool as proof that he had fulfilled his lonely mission.

Setting off from the inn, the man trudged over the moorland road to the meer. Upon nearing his destination, he was not a little startled by the cries of a woman appealing for help. Wondering whether it might be a trick of the mermaid attempting to lure him to his death, he hesitated, but was convinced of the reality of the voice. Pressing bravely forward, he found that a woman was being driven by a ruffianly fellow into the water in an attempt to drown her, in spite of her weak resistance and pleas for mercy. Suddenly, from out of the darkness, a masculine voice called, "Come Dick, Jack, Tom, here is the rogue we are wanting!" Whereupon the would-be murderer fled from the scene in a panic, and the woman —almost stripped of her clothing—was escorted back to the inn as evidence that her resourceful rescuer had won his wager. It transpired that the woman had previously been seduced by her cowardly attacker, and he, learning that she was in a state of pregnancy, had lured her to the lonely place with the intention of concealing one crime by committing another—murder!.

3. "Fair Flora"

Upon the verge of Grindle Moor, where winds
In vespers oftimes meet, and from the
Neighbouring woodlands seem to bring strange secrets from
Each soughing oak and whisking pine, the ruins
Of a little cot may yet be seen.
Anent its ruined walls, and looking o'er
The scene as 'twere, a marble statue stands.
Look! yonder is the figure sweet and fair,
As of an angel e'er was conjured in
The mind of man. Yea, 'tis the figure of
A lovely female, who, with one arm raised,
Points upwards to the sky, while in her hand
A rose of purest whiteness does she hold . . .

STANDING on a lonely hillside overlooking the village of Grindle-ford is a lonely statue of Flora, the Greek goddess of flowers. A strange place, you may think, to find the temple of a heathen deity. But there are no pagan altars, no shrine, no priests, no votaries and no temple. No libations are offered and no sacrifices made. There is no sound of praise or prayer—just the image of white stone. The sculptured figure has been sadly mutilated and defaced by acts of vandalism which culminated in its decapitation. Several times the head was replaced, but still the old Puritan instinct which condemns image worship—or sheer lust for wilful damage—asserted itself, and on each occasion the head was again forcibly dislodged. So now it is in the custody of a sympathetic resident who protects it from further damage or disfigurement, and the headless Flora stands in pitiful solitude, clasping her garland of cold stone flowers . . .

I remember when the site occupied by the statue was a moss-paved clearing at the head of an avenue of tall, stately trees, whose foliage was pierced here and there by shafts of sunlight which patterned the undergrowth with pools of greenish gold. The pewter-coloured trunks of beech trees rose on either side like living pillars supporting a vaulted arch of interlaced branches, forming a cathedral

17

aisle which could not but induce a sense of solemnity and reverence And the murmur of the wind among the leaves and the minstrelsy of birds conspired to create an atmosphere of music and magic. And the statue stood, dignified and regal, unharmed and unmolested by sacrilegious hands. Then came the wood-cutters with their timber drags, and soon the area was a scene of desolation, scarred by sawn-off boles and littered by an accumulation of tangled branches among which the felled trees lay like wooden goliaths slain on a field of battle. The mossy path was torn up by heavy wheels and trampling horses, and strewn with heaps of faggots and slices of sweet smelling wood fresh from the stroke of the axe. The statue was left in naked isolation, surveying the scene with melancholy eyes. After the wood-cutters came the vandals, but then once again a screen of trees wove garments of green to hide the nakedness of the statue from wanton eyes. Irreverent hands are seldom raised to add to the wounds suffered since it was transferred to this site from the grounds of nearby Stoke Hall.

Ever since its eviction from the Hall, the statue has been the subject of sinister stories—tales of murder and mystery. So tangled is the skein of these stories that one cannot unravel the confusion of threads to knit them into a discernible pattern. Some of the stories can be dismissed as mere fiction, and others can be analysed to extract their factual content; but even then it is impossible to arrive at a satisfactory evaluation of their claims to truth. Of one fact we can be certain: the statue came from Chatsworth. R. Murray Gilchrist wrote:- "Farther down the valley a strange 18th century house stands on a thickly wooded bank of the river. This is Stoke Hall, once the Peakland home of the Earls of Bradford. The neighbouring folk in former years used to tell a weird story of a skull that haunted the upper story, and one may be sure that they feared to pass alone after 'edge o' dark'. Although Stoke has no pretensions to architectural beauty, its position suggests romance and mystery. In the wood nearby stands a renaissance statue known as 'Fair Flora', a gift of the 'long-armed' Duke of Devonshire to a member of the Bridgeman family, but by popular belief a monument raised to the memory of a young lady who was murdered by a jealous lover."

A former member of the domestic staff at Stoke used to tell of an heiress to the property being murdered in the Hall, and spoke of indelible blood-stains and a haunted room in which neither members of the family, nor their guests, nor any of the servants were ever asked to sleep. Down by the wooded bank of the river Derwent —powdered white in February by a profusion of snowdrops—there is an old bathing-pool supplied by a tepid spring. Here a young man is said to have murdered his sweetheart.

There are stories told on the lighter side about the alleged haunting of the Hall. In the servants' quarters there was a rather gloomy passage, wide enough to drive a horse and cart along, with sculleries and other rooms leading off. Rustling noises and strange whispers were frequently heard in the passage, and such an atmosphere of fear and apprehension had been built up around the "haunted" passage that no one would enter after dark, and the position arose that the family had difficulty in retaining domestic staff. But one stout-hearted cook solved the mystery of the supernatural sounds by boldly flinging open the door to find scraps of paper fluttering along the draughty passage!

On another occasion a manservant, new to the service of the Hall, was introduced to the story of the ghost by regualr members of the staff who reinforced its reality by staging an "appearance." As the newcomer was ascending the stairs, he was terrified by a white figure gliding along the landing and, without a moment's hesitation, leaped over the banister to the hall below. Although he found that the mysterious figure was only a member of the staff draped in a white sheet, the initiation ceremony was too much for his nerves and he handed in his notice and abruptly departed.

I was told that the statue had been given to a Mrs. Taylor who had admired it when visiting Chatsworth. But with the statue came a spell of misfortune for the Hall and its occupants, and even the recipient of the gift, as she advanced in years, found its presence increasingly intolerable. As she looked on the dusky lawn in the evenings, or when the moon was silvering the landscape, the motionless statue assumed a ghostly quality, and this suggestion impressed itself so strongly upon Mrs. Taylor's imagination that its removal was deemed advisable to save her further distress.

And then rustic imagination took up the unfinished tale, claiming the statue as a memorial to a girl drowned in the swollen waters of the Derwent while eloping with her lover across the stepping-stones above Leadmill Bridge, or to a girl murdered by a band of gipsies. In a lengthy ballad entitled *The Astrologer's Daughter*, J. Castle Hall links the statue with a story he heard from an old gipsy who was camping in the vicinity. How much of the story was conceived in the imagination of the teller we cannot say, but the author explains in the preface:- "Many and varied are the local traditions touching the origin of this statue, each more or less romantic. But probably the story of an old gipsy near to the spot which she narrated to the writer excels alike in romance and antiquarian lore. The old hag was in company with other gipsies camping in the wood, and having noticed that a flower had been placed in the hand of the statue, I referred to the fact in conversation with the gipsy, when the latter, assuming a perfect acquaintance with the matter, told her strange tale. On this strange legend of the gipsy is founded *The Astrologer's Daughter*. And whether or not the story is altogether mythical, true it is that some hundred years ago there lived near Eyam an old man of extraordinary character, who was celebrated as an astrologer, as recorded in the works of Glover, Pendleton, and others, on the people and history of Derbyshire."

The poem tells of an astrologer and his daughter living in a lonely cottage, and sharing an interest in the pseudo-science which postulates the influence of the stellar bodies in the government of human life. This theme is developed in the poem. Victor, the son of a local squire, falls deeply in love with the girl and, when he is summoned for military service, they are married at her father's request by a friar from a neighbouring abbey. After a fleeting honeymoon, the reluctant husband leaves to take up his military assignment, and does not return for a prolonged period. Meanwhile:-

> *Twelve months have passed,*
> *And now the little cottage stands with door*
> *Ajar, and aspect wild and bare. Nor man*
> *Nor child the silence of its threshold breaks*
> *By day the haunt of birds whose fluttering wings*
> *Are overheard amongst the straggling leaves*
> *That now with mournful mien hang from its walls . . .*
> *Then Victor gave a sudden start, for there*
> *Before him stood fair Flora, clad in white!*
> *Yes, calm and beautiful beyond the power*
> *Of words to tell, she stood. Within her eyes*
> *There was sadness too unspeakable.*
> *But in a language far more sure than speech*
> *Those eyes revealed her soul's unchanged love.*
> *As Victor was about to speak and take*
> *Her hand in his, she moved aside, and by*
> *A gesture motioned Victor not to stir.*
> *Now points she to a glittering star that,*
> *Diamond-like, shines overhead.*
> *And then she forward leans, and Victor sees*
> *A gush of tears fall from her eyes upon*
> *A rose of purest whiteness that she holds*
> *Within her hand. No longer now he waits,*
> *But quickly clasps his hand around her form.*
> *O powers of mystery and mercy, help!*
> *His arms have through that outline passed as through*
> *A shadow . . .*

The sequel to the story was that Flora, worried and anxious at the prolonged absence of her husband, had died leaving a baby daughter which, when Victor had recovered from the shattering blow, became a source of comfort and consolation to help compensate him for the shortness of his married life.

After I had spoken on Derbyshire ghost stories to members of Hathersage W.I., a member made an incidental enquiry about

Fair Flora. After I had briefly recounted the several legends with which I was familiar, she added a further version. A young lady at Stoke Hall had fallen in love with a youth of lower social degree, and her parents gave the couple to understand that they had other intentions for the daughter's future marital relations than those they had planned for themselves. To prevent any violation of these plans, the girl was securely locked in an upstairs room of the mansion but, with the connivance of her lover, she made her escape. Her flight, however, was soon discovered and a pursuit was immediately organised. The eloping couple had only reached the site of the statue when the girl was shot dead—either by accident or design —on the spot, and the marble figure was placed there as memorial of the sad event.

Tilley (*Old Halls and Manors of Derbyshire*) has a story of one former owner of Stoke Hall:- "There is a tradition told of William Cavendish, Duke of Newcastle, while Lord of Stoke, that during the night following his taking possession of Bradford, for the King, from the Parliamentarians, the ghost of a lady appeared to him and said 'Spare poor Bradford'. And when he rose and gave the order that no life should be taken, the spirit vanished, blessing him. History shows that he and his troops left the town during the next day, to the joy of the inhabitants. Many of us frequently pass Stoke Hall and never remember the man whose figure was foremost in those sad conflicts when liberty fought loyalty at such a frightful cost and sacrifice."

And so the statue of Fair Flora stands, mute and mutilated. Pale, silvery grey lichen patterns the flowing folds of her weathered stone robes, with here and there a splash of the golden variety eating into the surface of the stone. Early in the year, one may perhaps find a few snowdrops—the "fair maids of February"—clustering around her feet, and in summer the golden ragwort and pink willow herb grow around the pedestal on which she stands. And to those who may venture up the avenue in the clear light of the moon, she stands like the headless wraith of a bride waiting at an invisible altar for the groom who never comes.

4. Chronicles of the Crusades

Few stories in the library of legend are so rich in religious romance and interest as those which have survived from the days of the Crusades. They tell of miracle and mysticism, of heroism and adventure; of epic battles fought by patriots of the Christian faith. The visitor to old churches may sometimes find in an obscure corner, perhaps mottled by the pastel tints created by sunlight filtering through a stained glass window, the ancient alabaster effigy of some cross-legged knight, clasping his heart in his hands to remind the onlooker that, although his dust mingles with the sacred soil of Palestine, his embalmed heart lies buried in the church of his homeland. And although the monument may be scratched with the graffiti of irreverent vandals, and may have been mutilated by bygone Puritans, it brings to life the stories of fairy-tale castles and armour-clad knights mounted on proud horses bearing fluttering pennants embroidered with the motif of the red cross.

Some of the warriors who survived those far distant campaigns returned with souvenirs of their visit. Sir Geoffrey Finderne brought back a narcissus which was propogated in his native village of Finderne, and which long survived the extinction of his family and the demolition of his ancestral home. At another Derbyshire village, Syrian daffodils bloomed each spring to keep alive the memory of a Crusader who had brought back the parent bulbs. The warriors' exploits have long been forgotten, but generations of fragrant flowers have scented the breezes for centuries to link the far-off past with the present.

According to an ancient document entitled *The Severed Hand of Johanne with the Long Hair: a Legend of Knowle Hills and Anchor Church*, a certain Sir Hugo and Lady Johanne de Burdett lived in a now vanished castle at Knowle Hills about the middle of the 12th century. They had been married by parental arrangement rather than by personal choice, but Sir Hugo and his wife were happily matched, and Eleanor, wife of King Henry II, is said to have often remarked to her husband, "There are few couples in your domain who set so good an example as Sir Hugo and his Johanne."

The atmosphere of connubial joy was chilled by the occasional

22

visits of the Baron of Boyvill, a distant relative of Sir Hugo, who lived in the vicinity of Castleton. His conversation largely concerned the romance and military glamour of the Crusades, and his glowing accounts excited such interest in his kinsman that the Lady Johanne feared instinctively that her husband would be tempted to join the increasing number of knights responding to the challenge of the Holy War. Little did Sir Hugo realise that the scheming Baron had an evil motive in seeking to inspire his allegiance to the Crusaders' cause, and that his interest in the outcome was far from being indifferent or impersonal. But the Lady Johanne made it obvious that she was displeased at the subtle influence he had exerted over her husband.

Having succeeded in creating a spirit of uneasiness and dissatisfaction in Sir Hugo's chivalrous heart, the wily Baron began to reduce the number of his visits, but arranged to keep him well informed of events with messages sent by a travelling friar named Father Bernard who had frequent occasion to visit the Monastery of Black Canons at Repton. Often Sir Hugo's mind was troubled and his patience vexed as he listened at the monastery gate to the exciting tales of battles being waged in the Holy Land, and he would reproach himself with such thoughts as, "Here I am wasting my youth and allowing my sword to rust in idleness, chained by the beauty of a woman—when in the presence of Johanne I have no power to leave her—it is only in her absence I feel free to think. I will consult the Holy Father and be guided by his advice."

As the result of this interview, Sir Hugo was counselled to spurn the comforts and luxuries of home, and overrule the domestic conditions which had hitherto restrained him from dedicating his sword to the cause which lay so near his heart. The friar supplied him with a sleeping draught to administer to his wife, lest she should weaken his resolution and cause him to rescind his decision to accept the challenge. And so, one morning when she awakened from her drugged sleep, Johanne was saddened to find a golden heart—inscribed "five years"—hanging around her neck. Sir Hugo had joined the Crusade!

For three years the Lady Johanne patiently watched and waited for news of her absent husband, beguiling the weary hours by embroidering a wonderful altar cloth for the shrine of Our Lady of Repton. Its threads of silver and gold were interwoven with her own long hair, and its design portrayed birds and insects, fruits and flowers in exquisite detail. One day it was to be dedicated, she planned, as a thank-offering for her husband's safe return. But the day came when her hopes were shattered, for Father Bernard brought the dread news that Sir Hugo had been taken prisoner and was being held to ransom by the Turks. With all speed the anxious wife despatched sufficient gold to secure the knight's release and restoration.

Day by day, and week by week, the Lady Johanne kept vigil, yearning for tidings of her husband's safety, until about a year later she saw an armed figure riding up the avenue and into the courtyard. On his breast was the symbol and sign of the Crusades— a red cross. But, to her dismay, she found that it was the Baron de Boyvill who broke the news that Sir Hugo's dead body had been handed over in exchange for the ransom she had provided. The grief-stricken widow was offered little comfort and sympathy by the Baron who went on to inform her that, in view of the fact that Sir Hugo had left no heir, the estate would become his property. She was, however, given the opportunity of retaining possession on the condition that she became his wife; an ultimatum which she promptly and proudly rejected, and as a result of which she was held a prisoner in her own castle until the expiration of five years. In those days the rights of individuals—even in the higher levels of society—were less clearly defined than today, and the dispossession of personal liberty or estate by legal misrepresentation, or by the exercise of ruthless force, was by no means an uncommon experience.

When the period had elapsed, the fair captive was informed that she was to become the baron's bride and that he had set out that very morning to summon his friends, to the marriage ceremony. Suddenly the door was flung open and, to the amazement of Johanne, she was confronted by her husband. But, instead of being received into his arms in joyous reunion, she saw that his countenance was distorted by mingled rage and hatred as he cried, "Unfaithful woman, betrayer of thy husband, thy hour of punishment is at hand". Drawing his sword and seizing her left arm, he added the terrible words, "This hand on which I placed the bridal ring shall be the sacrifice of thy infidelity, and thus I immolate my revenge." Without further explanation, and denying his wife the opportunity to speak in her own defence, the impassioned knight struck one blow and severed her arm as she fell bleeding at his feet. Having committed this terrible deed, Sir Hugo turned and strode away, returning later to live in morose and melancholy solitude.

But there was a sequel to the story, for a messenger arrived one night with an urgent message imploring Sir Hugo to visit the religious recluse who lived in the cavern retreat known as Anchor Church. It was said that this hermit had so punished himself with penances that his cries had been heard from afar, and had been construed as evidence of his exceeding piety; so much so that pilgrims came to visit him because of the miracles he was reputed to perform. When Sir Hugo reached the grotto, he found the hermit lying at the point of death, terribly tortured by his conscience and begging the knight's pardon for a great and terrible crime committed against him and his late wife. Having been assured of the knight's forgiveness, he handed Sir Hugo a parchment and

24

died. Unable to read, the latter hastened to Repton where a monk unfolded the contents of the parchment:-

"The mendicant monk friar Bernard and the recluse of the Trent are one and the same. Worldly vanity seduced me to crime—I wished to be thought a saint and I have been a wretched sinner. I travelled over Europe to gain partisans to the cause. I gathered money and spent it in wickedness instead of charity. The Baron of Boyvill paid me to gain over Sir Hugo de Burdett and I accompany'd both to the Holy Land. I betrayed Sir Hugo into the Paynim's hands and after obtaining money for his ransom from his lady, I returned with the sum which I shared with the Baron; and found means to let Sir Hugo know that his lady was false and refused to ransom him. After this the Baron came back to England and endeavoured by representing that her husband was dead to induce the lady Johanne to become his wife, which she steadfastly refused I had obtained large sums from the Baron, but of late he had refused to give me more and in the end I wrought his ruin. I procured the release of Sir Hugo by my agents and sent him word that his wife and friend were both false. He encountered the Baron in the woods of Foremark and slew him, for he taunted him with having gained the affections of his wife. Mad with jealousy, Sir Hugo put the innocent lady to death. Remorse almost drove me distracted when I found the effect of my work, and I strove by penitence to atone for my dreadful sins and those I had caused. Pray for my soul, and let masses be said for one otherwise lost for ever."

Sir Hugo's heart was filled with unspeakable grief and remorse as he returned to his home and, for the first time since her death, he entered his wife's room and found the embroidered altar cloth and the golden heart he had hung about her neck on the night of his departure to the Holy Land. Tradition tells how the mourning husband was led by the song of a nightingale from his wife's grave in the castle courtyard, until he reached Ancote in Warwickshire and there built a monastery in expiation of his crime. And, when it was completed, the cloth of silver, gold and hair embroidery was draped upon the altar, and people suffering from maladies of the hand resorted thither for centuries to be miraculously healed of their afflictions.

At Ridgeway Farm, Repton, two quaintly carved stone heads are preserved. Originally there were three, and they stood on a wall at Knowle Hills. They are said to represent the principal actors in this ancient drama of the Lady Johanne, for the narrative concludes:- "and all that remains of the old building is now formed into a pleasure house—where usually not a sound is heard but the wind among the old trees, and the rustle of the ivy waving to and fro along the old wall, where you see that strange face carved, that seems as if it were looking over the battlements, watching what is going on. Some say on moonlight nights the whole figure has been seen, and it looks like a knight in armour as it walks in stately step, all round this green, where once stood a tower, and it pauses at a little doorway, utters a deep sigh and vanishes . . . There were two old women who once lived here and they used to hear and see strange things, chains rattling, and screams and groans that were awful. One of the old women died and used to come back to the other and tell wonderful secrets, so she said. But she went, too, and nothing out of the common ever happens now."

*   *   *   *   *

For many years Sutton Hall, near Chesterfield, has stood a gaunt and roofless ruin; a mausoleum in which proud memories lay buried and forgotten. Its gardens and grounds have been a wilderness of weeds and tangled undergrowth where gardeners once tended smooth lawns and rose beds, and where the topiarist demonstrated his skill. Once the peacock strutted proudly across its lawns and terraces; fountains erupted plumes of water into stone basins that became broken and dry, and pools where the stately swan once glided amongst floating water-lilies became stagnant and choked with weeds. Where there had been dignity there was desolation; where there was once bustle and activity, there was the silence of the tomb. Time had changed the very face of the landscape, for instead of parks there were pits, and instead of the huntsman and his hounds you might find the collier and his courser; instead of the falconer and his hawk the foundryman and his basket of pigeons: what had once been the estate of a nobleman became an estate for the housing of many families.

This partially demolished Hall, belonging in latter years to the Arkwrights, occupied the site of a much older mansion; a hall once garrisoned by a staunch Royalist named Francis Leake who was created a baronet in 1611 and Lord Deincourt in 1624. During the Civil War this mansion was besieged by a force of 500 men equipped with three pieces of ordnance, who were under the command of Colonel Thomas Gell. Deincourt and his men were taken prisoner, but the master of the house was released upon giving an assurance that he would, within eight days, repair to Derby and submit himself to the censure of Parliament. But the promise was never fulfilled and the recalcitrant nobleman joined the royal troops at Newark. In 1645 he was created Earl of Scarsdale. Remaining loyal to the Crown after the collapse of the royal cause, the Earl manifested his contempt of Parliament by refusing to pay composition for his estates. These were sequestered and sold, but were redeemed by his friends for £18,000. After the execution of the King, he "became so much mortified that he apparelled himself frequently in sackcloth, and, causing his grave to be digged some years before his death, laid himself down in it every Friday, exercising himself frequently in divine meditation and prayer."

One of the ancestors of this Earl, who lived in ancient Sutton

Hall, figured in another Derbyshire story of the Crusades. The name of this warrior who joined the militant pilgrims pledged to rescue the sacred sites from pagan desecration was Sir Nicholas Leake and, before bidding farewell to Derbyshire, he and his wife broke a ring between them as a pledge of their mutual fidelity. During a battle with the Turks, Sir Nicholas was captured and detained for many years in expectation of a ransom. Weary and dispirited by his long imprisonment, the knight fervently prayed for deliverance, making a solemn vow that if he was restored to his wife and home in Derbyshire, he would make ample provision for the poor of his parish. And then he fell asleep. The next morning he awakened to find himself in the porch of Sutton church and lost no time in making his way to the Hall. But here the dishevelled knight was treated with suspicion, for the years of confinement had wrought considerable change in his features, and his clothing was tattered and torn. The servants mistook him for some impostor who had heard that their master was missing and long mourned as dead, and who was seeking to impersonate him in order to claim possession of wife, house and estate. And so his request for an audience with their mistress was repeatedly refused and he was driven away from the door with threats of imprisonment. Then he remembered the broken ring and pleaded that the servants would take it to their mistress, and when this was done the ring was immediately recognised and the two halves were found to fit perfectly together. Then followed a joyous reunion and many years of happiness.

Nor did Sir Nicholas forget the vow he had made in captivity. In gratitude for his miraculous deliverance, he made provision in his will for eight bushels of wheat to be baked into loaves and given to the poor of Sutton, Duckmanton and Temple Normanton each St. Nicholas Day. Francis, Lord Deincourt, increased the dole which was distributed in 2 lb. loaves each year until the death in 1736 of Nicholas Leake, the last Earl of Scarsdale.

The above tradition has been incorporated in a ballad written by Richard Howitt, but the poet appears to have combined the story of the Royalist Sir Nicholas with that of his Crusading ancestor. The following verses concern the legend of the broken ring:-

Oft before the cross, the altar,
  Murmuring prayers he sinks to rest;
To his God, and to his Saviour—
  And the Virgin Mother blest.

And for love unto the Virgin
  Finds in Heaven his prayer chief grace!
"Mary, Mother, me deliver,
  From the horrors of this place!"

There his patrimonial mansion
  He beheld in moonlight sleep,
Saw with joy, though mystery veiled it—
  Sadness and a silence deep.

And, O miracle of gladness!
  More, those ancient legends say,
Was permitted him to witness,
  Waking in the open day.

In his old church-porch awaking—
  Trance, or voyage all unknown;
O'er his own domains he wandered—
  Saw and knew them for his own . . .

Age rejoices; in the Mansion
  Rural hinds find wassail cheer;
And bright troops of Knights and Ladies,
  Crowd the Hall from far and near.

Who is this in weeds unseemly,
  Half a man that seems, half beast,
Who obtrudes himself unbidden
  On the merry marriage feasts?

Hermit is he, or some Pilgrim,
  Entering boldly his own cell?
No—he lacks those ancient symbols,
  Sandal-shoon, and scallop shell.

All the youngsters titter; anger
  Flushes cheeks austere and cold:
Whilst the aged look complacent
  On a beggar that is bold.

"Bear this Ring unto your Mistress,"
  To a page Sir Francis cried;
And his words emphatic uttered
  Rung throughout the dwelling wide.

Pensive in her room, the Matron
  —Grieved—but distant from the crowd;
She would not with selfish sorrow
  Their bright countenances cloud.

There her Ring receiving; Lucy
  Knew the sender of her gift,
And,it seemed, by feet unaided,
  To him she descended swift.

There upon the rugged stranger,
  Gazed, with momentary check,
Gazed, but for a passing moment,
  And then fell upon his neck.

*   *   *   *   *

Another story from this age of miracles concerns the crumbling ruins of Eastwood Old Hall, near Ashover; a landmark which was made the target of Parliamentary prejudice. There is a striking similarity between this legend and that of Sir Francis Leake, for it tells how a wife was saved from innocently committing bigamy while under the impression that she was a widow. While wedding-bells pealed across the meadows of Ashover, a shackled knight was being miraculously transported from his place of exile to his native Derbyshire.

The legend concerns a member of the Reresby family, and one of the documents relating to this old family recalls the fact that hermits once retired to Ashover parish to spend their lives in fasting. prayer and holy contemplation. The deed says:- "15th Aug. 1319. Ralph de Rerisby, son of Robert, conveyed to Godfrey del Stubbynges, in Essovere, lands called 'le Hermite Ker' (*the Hermite land*) lying in the territory del Stubbynge." An earlier reference to the same place is contained in a 13th century conveyance stating that Walter, the Abbot of Dale Abbey, conveyed to Richard Venator, Bosco de Morwde "where hermits formerly dwelt."

J. Tilley records the Reresby legend as follows:- "It is related that one of the Reresbys, named Leonard—soon after they had located themselves at Ashover—that 'serving his Prince in the Holy War was taken prisoner by the Saracens and there detained captive nearly seven years; that his wife, according to the laws of the land, was afterwards married to another; that being apprehensive of this accident, by the power of prayer he was miraculously delivered and insensibly conveyed with shackles and gyves, or fetters, upon his limbs, and laid upon the East Hill, in Thriburgh Field, as the bell was being tolled for his wife's second marriage, which her first husband's return prevented, though he presently died as soon as brought into the church, where he desired to pay his first visit,' The shackles with which he was bound (the tradition says) were preserved at Thriburgh for generations and eventually made into ploughshares about the time of Henry VIII."

5. The Devil and Deepdale

The devil, one night, as he chanced to sail
In a stormy wind, by the abbey of Dale,
Suddenly stopp'd, and look'd wild with surprise,
That a structure so fair in that valley should rise:
When last he was there it was lonely and still;
And the hermitage scoop'd in the side of the hill,
With its wretched old inmate his beads a-telling,
Were all could be found of life, dweller, and dwelling.
The hermit was seen in the rock no more;
The nettle and dock had sprung up at the door;
And each window the fern and the hart's-tongue hung o'er.
Within, 'twas dampness and nakedness all:
The Virgin ,as fair and holy a block
As ever yet stood in a niche of a rock,
Had fallen to the earth, and was broke in the fall.

(William and Mary Howitt)

THE monastic remains of Derbyshire are so few that they can almost be counted on one hand, and little remains to remind us of their erstwhile grandeur. Repton Priory is absorbed in a school, and Darley Abbey—once the largest and most important—has little to recall its 12th century magnificence. Beauchief was the best preserved, but was abducted by Yorkshire, and at Dale a slender arch serrated with broken tracery stands in dignified solitude like a stone sentinel guarding the sacred site. Well might Richard Howitt say:-

With that one arch before thee set—
That one old abbey-window fair;
The only wreck of the rich fane
That restless time would spare.

Excavations at Dale Abbey have revealed foundations of the nave, choir, transepts, two chapels, and the chapter house. Parts of the refectory wall, kitchen and gateway can also be traced in adjacent buildings. One of its treasures is the sculptured representa-

Dale Abbey arch, and the tiny village church dovetailed into a farmhouse.

tion of a canon in his robes, and holding a book. When his grave was opened, it was found to contain a great oak coffin in which lay a skeleton reposing on a bed of leaves which were still green after 500 years of inhumation. I like to think that this was the tomb of Thomas de Muscova who recorded the outstanding events in the history of the Abbey in his *Chronicle;* a document which has Biblical style of language and presentation. The text of the document forms an acrostic, in that the opening initial of each section supplies one of the letters of the writer's name.

Some of the old timberwork from the abbey can be seen at Radbourne church, while Morley possesses some of its stone window frames and 15th century painted glass depicting scenes concerning the apocryphal dispute caused when the monks were accused of shooting deer in the royal forest. The incident of the king's grant of an area of land, the extent of which was determined by its being ploughed round with deer in one day, is also portrayed. Another scene shows a monk admonishing a manacled brother who had been guilty of some misdemeanour.

Describing a visit to the Abbey over a century ago, Dr. Spencer T. Hall wrote:- "Not far off, though in another quarter, and partly formed of a remnant of the Abbey, is the old Manor-house—a mere cottage in appearance, and yet to this day the place in which the manor courts are held. A little door inside is made of a beautifully carved piece of wood, which, when new, had probably occupied a much more dignified place in the monastery. And it is not until the visitor has wandered somewhat freely about, that he is aware how many relics of the old foundation are in-built with the dwellings of the people . . ."

In the following extract from his *Chronicle*, Thomas de Muscova records his call to the separated life of the monastery, and introduces the abbot and several brethren who made a deep impression upon his life:- "Being in the middle of the flowery period of boyhood and youth given by my father to the service of God and of his pious Virgin Mother, I took upon myself the sacred habit in this place from the abbot, John Gauncorth, a venerable father, lovely in the eyes of God and men, who had been the especial associate of the blessed Augustine, of Lavendon. These two shone forth, in their days and in their orders, like the morning and evening stars in the firmament of heaven. There were at that time, men belonging to this monastery, who lived before the Lord without enmity, who wore the vestments of virtue, who had the countenances of the angels, who glowed with mutual affection, and served the Lord Jesus Christ devoutly. Who is there capable of enumerating the virtues of the friar Galfrid of Sawell, of the friar Roger of Derby, or of the rest? It became such a father to have such sons."

In the third chapter, Thomas tells of the Derby baker who, after a life of piety and religious devotion, was vouchsafed a vision in which he felt called to further spiritual discipline by living in isolation to serve God in meditation and prayer. He tells how the recluse excavated a cavern-like hermitage from the sandstone rock in Deepdale:-

"There was a baker in Derby, in the street which is called after the name of St. Mary . . . And this baker, otherwise called Cornelius, was a religious man, fearing God, and moreover so wholly occupied in good works and the bestowing of alms, that whatsoever remained to him on every seventh day beyond what had been required for the clothing of himself and his, and the needful things of the house, he would on the Sabbath-day, take to the church of St. Mary, and give to the poor for the love of God and of the Holy Virgin. And when he had during many years led a life of such pious exercises as these, and was dear to God and accepted by him, it pleased God to try him more perfectly, and having tried him to crown him with glory. And thereupon it happened, that on a certain day in autumn, when he had resigned himself to repose at the hour of noon, the Blessed Virgin Mary appeared to him in his sleep, saying 'Acceptable in the eyes of my Son and of me, are the alms thou hast bestowed. But now, if thou art willing to be made perfect, leave all that thou

"Fair Flora" prior to decapitation (chapter 3).

Stoke Hall, where the statue of "Fair Flora" stood for many years (chapter 3).

Anchor Church, where the penitent friar Bernard died (chapter 4).

Repton, for whose church an altar cloth was embroidered with her own hair by the Lady Johanne (chapter 4).

Sutton Scarsdale Hall, home of the Leakes (chapter 4).

hast, and go to Deepdale, where thou shalt serve my son and me in solitude; and when thou shalt happily have terminated thy course, thou shalt inherit the kingdom of love, joy, and eternal bliss which God has prepared for those who love him. The man awakening, perceived the divine goodness which had been done for his sake, and giving thanks to God and the Blessed Virgin, his encourager, he straightway went forth without speaking a word to anyone; *with knowledge ignorant*, to use the expression of St. Benedict: *with knowledge*, because he had been taught the name of the place; *ignorant*, because he knew not where any place of that name might be.

"Having turned his steps towards the east, it befell him as he was passing through the middle of the village of Stanley, he heard a woman say to a girl:: 'Take our calves with you: drive them as far as Deepdale, and make haste back.' Having heard this, this man, admiring the favour of God, and believing that this word had been spoken in grace, as it were, to him, was astonished, and approached nearer and said, 'Good woman, tell me, where is Depedale?' She replied, 'Go with this maiden, and she, if you desire it, will show you that place.' When he had arrived there, he found that the place was marshy and of fearful aspect, far distant from any habitation of man. Then directing his steps to the south-east of the place, he cut for himself in the side of the mountain, in the rock, a very small dwelling, and an altar towards the south, which hath been preserved unto this day; and there he served God, day and night, in hunger and thirst, in cold and in meditation."

Chapter five tells of the hermit, having been given the land and tithe of the mill of Burgum (Borrowash) by the generous Adulph, Lord of the Manor, vacating his cave and building a house and oratory upon the site of which now stands the tiny church:-

"And it came to pass that the old designing enemy of mankind, beholding this disciple of Christ flourishing with the different flowers of virtues, began to envy him, as he envies other holy men; sending frequently amidst his cogitations the vanities of the world, the bitterness of his existence, the solitariness of his situation, and the various troubles of the desert; as Humfrid, and many persons now living, understood and were accustomed to relate to me and to others. But the aforesaid man of God, conscious of the venom of the crooked serpent, did by continual prayer and repeated fastings and holy meditations, cast forth, through the grace of God, all his temptations. Whereupon the enemy rose upon him in all his might both secretly and openly, waging with him a visible conflict. And while the assaults of his foe became day by day more grievous, he had to sustain a very great want of water. Wandering about the neighbouring places, he discovered a spring, in a valley, not far from his dwelling, towards the west, and near unto it he made for himself a cottage, and built an oratory in honour of God and the Blessed Virgin. There wearing away the sufferings of his life, laudably, in the service of God, he departed happily to God, from out of the prison house of the body."

The sixth chapter deals with the vision of the golden cross:-"There was one Uthlagus, a very famous man, who frequented these parts, on account of the passage of wayfarers through the forest between Nottingham and Derby: for the whole country between the bridge of Derby and the water of . . . was at that time covered with wood. And it came to pass, on one of the days of the summer season, this Uthlagus was sitting upon Lynderyke, which is a hill westward of the gate of our monastery, with his companions amusing themselves around him, when a deep sleep fell upon him. And, while he slept, he saw in a dream, a golden cross, standing in that spot, where the foundations of our church is laid, the top of which touched the heavens: while the extremities of the arms stretched themselves to each side, even unto the ends of the world. And moreover he beheld men coming from various nations of the earth, and most devoutly adoring that cross.

"The man being aroused and awakened from his sleep, called together his companions, and related to them the vision that had been revealed to him from the Lord; and he added and said, 'Truly, my dearly beloved companions, the valley which ye behold below and which is contiguous to this eminence, is a holy place.' 'Of a truth,' he said again, 'the Lord is in this place, and I know him not. Children shall be born and shall grow up, and shall declare to their children the wonderful works that the Lord will perform in this valley. This valley, I say unto you, shall be white with the flowers of virtues, and shall be filled with delights and plenteousness. For there shall come, as it hath been revealed to me, from various nations, to worship the Lord, in this valley, and to serve him, until the end of time through the succession of ages. And because our Lord Jesus Christ hath deigned to show to me, a sinner, his secret intentions, so shall ye understand that ye can no longer have in me, either a companion or a leader; but aided by his grace, I will amend my life according to his will.' Then embracing them every one, he turned himself away from them; but whither he went, nought was known at that time concerning him . . ."

What happened to this converted bandit after he had renounced his life of lawlessness and deserted his former followers is a blank chapter, but it was assumed that he went to Deepdale and there—in penitence and prayer—found forgiveness, reconciliation and spiritual peace by living in communion with God. Later chapters of the *Chronicle* tell of the occupation of Deepdale by members of several monastic orders. They tell of members of the community suffering privation and want, and of others neglecting their solemn vows. There were times marked by a lessening of the intensity of faith and fervour; times when discipline was relaxed, regulations ignored, abuses committed and condoned, and a gradual vitiation of the former high standards of conduct. Some of the monks were guilty of poaching deer in the royal forest, and one of the priors became notorious for his skill in making counterfeit coins. He also committed a serious breach of moral etiquette by consorting for immoral purposes with a woman of Morley and, when summoned by his superiors to account for his degrading behaviour, committed suicide by bleeding himself to death in a hot bath.

The monastery was variously occupied by the canons of de la Kalc, Tupholme, Welbeck and Newhouse. Built in or about the year 1204, it was surrendered to the Crown on October 20th, 1539. After the Dissolution, the site and demesnes of the Abbey were leased to Francis Pole who purchased the altar, crucifix, organ, gravestones and all the live and dead stock. The day had come—contrary to the prediction of Uthlagus—that the Abbey was deserted. The lamps were extinguished and the altar candles had flickered out. There was no longer the chanting of psalms, the intoning of prayers, or the perfume of incense. The building was stripped of its furnishings and slowly reduced to a state of ruin.

But God is still worshipped in the tiny church—renowned as the smallest in Derbyshire—which once shared its thatched roof with the pilgrim's inn. This rather strange blend of sacred and secular architecture still continues, except that the inn has been converted into a dwelling-house. And pilgrims still come from all nations, as Uthlagus said they would, perhaps not so much to worship as to wonder. And among the many pilgrims, artists have come with sketch-book, paints and easel, and these probably included Joseph Wright from nearby Derby, whose enigmatic painting, "A river scene", appears to be a portrayal of the abbey with more extensive ruins. For many years the picture was thought to be the work of Richard Wilson and it was not until the first half of the present century that it was identified as the work of Wright.

Before concluding this story of Dale Abbey, the reader may be interested in William and Mary Howitt's satirical account of the reaction of that "designing old enemy of mankind" to the deer-stealing episode:-

The devil he heard, the devil he flew
Away in a whirlwind, that tore as it blew,
Rocks and houses, vast forests of oaks,
And buried some hundreds of cattle and folks.
Then chattered each pane in those windows high,
As the fiend arose in the act to fly;
Then a terrible gust did those towers assail,
As the fiend set off from the Abbey of Dale.
He summon'd his imps in the height of his spleen,
And question'd how many at Dale had been;
And what were the doings might there be seen?

One had seen plenty of beef and beer;
One had been with the friar a-chasing the deer;
One had carried out venison to twenty good wives,
And had wonder'd to see the monks handle their knives,
O'er the smoking hot pasties and sparkling ale,
By the snug evening fires in the village of Dale.
Many had been at a maid's confessing,
And some, when St. Robert conferr'd his blessing
On pious old souls, that to heaven would sail
By giving their lands to the Abbey of Dale.
Some, of the shrine of our lady told,
Of the relics, and jewels, and coffers of gold;
But all of them dwelt on the bountiful cheer,
How jocundly flew the whole round of the year,
But chief when the monks were a-chasing the deer.

The devil no longer such tidings could brook;
He started and stamp'd till his hot dwelling shook:
'O ho!' quoth he, to the demon powers,
'These knavish monks are no monks of ours;
They travel to heaven with feast and song,
And absolve each other while going along.
But troth! if I yet have a subject on earth,
I'll spoil their hunting—I'll mar their mirth!'
He flew to the keepers, the keepers they pace
Away to Sir Gilbert, the lord of the chase;
Sir Gilbert de Grendon he sped to the king,
And with grievous complaints made his proud palace ring:
How the friars at Dale forsook missal and mass,
To chant o'er a bottle, or shrive a lass;
No matins bell call'd them up in the morn,
But the yell of the hounds, and the sound of the horn;
No penance the monk in his cell could stay,
But a broken leg or a rainy day;
The pilgrim that came to the Abbey door,
With the feet of the fallow deer found it nail'd o'er;
The pilgrim that into the kitchen was led,
On Sir Gilbert's venison there was fed,
And saw skins and antlers hang o'er his head.
The king was wroth, and with angry tone
He ordered St. Robert before his throne:
St. Robert appear'd in three weeks and a day,
For hot was the weather, and long was the way,
He spoke so wisely, he pleaded so well,
That the king, in sooth, had trouble to tell
Which of the two that before him came
To the forest and deer had the fairest claim.

But the devil, who sat behind the throne,
At that did inwardly writhe and groan,
And whisper'd into the royal ear,
'St. Robert is famous for taming the deer.'
Then sprang the king gaily up from his throne,
And spoke that fancy, and deem'd it his own;
'For taming of deer St. Robert is famed;
Go catch the wild stags, and get them tamed;
With wood, water, and game, as much forest ground
As with such brave steeds thou canst plough round
While two summer suns through the heavens do sail,
Shall for ever belong to the Abbey of Dale:
But if set those two suns ere thou circle the same,
They shall cancel for ever and ever thy claim.'
Sir Gilbert frown'd—St. Robert look'd gay,
But the envious devil went laughing away."

6.   The Mandrake Tree

IF some of Derbyshire's trees had the gift of articulation claimed for their species by Shakespeare, their wooden tongues would have some strange stories to tell. And, as a matter of fact (or fiction), tradition alleges that one of them had the faculty of speech and another screamed with pain at the blow of an axe or the incision of a knife. Trees have been—and, in some instances, still remain —landmarks in Derbyshire history.

Near Bradwell, the place-name of Eddentree marks the legendary site of a tree upon which a Saxon king named Edwin suffered the sentence of death by hanging. The tree has long since vanished, but the name remains to identify the spot where the regicides carried out their summary execution. Gore Lane and Deadman's Clough are said to be place-names recalling the same period.

In the parish of Wormhill, an ash marked the site of a cottage where James Brindley, the canal engineer, was born in 1716. After the cottage had been deserted by its last tenant, it fell into a state of ruin and disrepair. The roof caved in and the walls crumbled, and the seedling of an ash grew between the crevices of the slabs of stone which had paved the floor, forcing them apart and growing into a stout tree. So that, when all other vestiges of masonry and timber had disappeared, Brindley's Tree kept alive the birthplace site of the illiterate genius who had made so great a contribution to commercial and industrial progress during the 18th century, and had earned the tribute from Thomas Carlyle:- "The English are a dumb people. They can do great acts but not describe them. Whatsoever of strength the man had in him will be written in the work he does. The rugged Brindley has little to say for himself. He has chained seas together. His ships do visibly float over valleys, and invisibly through the hearts of mountains; the Mersey and the Thames, the Humber and the Severn, have shaken hands." The original tree has long since disappeared, but another has been planted in its place.

Another tree which began its career as a seedling sown by chance still flourishes in the orchard of an inn at King's Newton, near Melbourne. Like a foundling it was carefully removed from the thatch of the village inn, the Hardinge Arms, and tenderly nursed by the landlord who was keenly interested in horticulture. Recognising it as the seedling of an apple, he transferred it to a plant-pot and eventually to his orchard. The growing sapling was carefully cultivated and developed into a healthy tree, becoming parent of one of the most popular varieties of apple we may purchase from our green-grocer—the Newton Wonder; a name which might well be mistaken as having some connection with Sir Isaac Newton and his discovery of the principle of gravity.

Proud, yet lonely, another famous tree crowns the summit of Oaker Hill, near Matlock. Unlike the foregoing trees, this was planted with a purpose and remains as a memorial to the person who planted it. Its story lives on in literature and has provoked the muse of several poets, including that of William Wordsworth who blended its ingredients of romance and pathos into the alchemy of one of his lesser known sonnets which begins:-

> *'Tis said that to the brow of yon fair hill*
> *Two brothers clomb; and turning face to face,*
> *Nor one look more exchanging, grief to still*
> *Or feed, each planted on that lofty place*
> *A chosen tree . . . ,*

This lonely tree has been portrayed in the pastel shades of stained glass and can be seen incorporated in the design of a war memorial window in the neighbouring church of South Darley.

The story goes that two brothers named Shore, who belonged to the family from which Florence Nightingale sprang, each planted a tree on the summit of the hill before setting off in opposite directions to seek their fortunes. One of them was successful and returned a wealthy man to find that his tree had also prospered. The other was less fortunate, dying prematurely; and, as though due to some strange telepathic coincidence, his tree began to wilt and wither and also died, leaving the surviving twin to mourn its loss in solitude. Other companion trees are said to have been planted on special occasions, but have never flourished.

Only a little distance away is the venerable Darley Yew which claims to be the oldest inhabitant of the churchyard, and perhaps the oldest tree in the county. One writer says that it has been more photographed than many a film-star and more paragraphed than many a politician. A local poet named Gisbourne sang its praises and John Holland made it the subject of a sonnet. This tree was painted in oils by David Cox junior, and I remember seeing the picture included in an exhibition of paintings displayed in a Sheffield art gallery to illustrate the skills and techniques of the picture restorer. Some of the exhibits had a square, others a circle or rectangle, of picture which had been treated to remove the accumulated dust and grime from the threads of the canvas, bringing back the original warmth and beauty of the colours as when they were first transferred from the palette by the gentle caress of the artist's brush. The one by Cox gave the impression of a clean finger stroked down a grimy window pane to reveal the hidden charm of a distant landscape. Since then it has been completely renovated to show the sunlit scene as it was first seen through the eyes of the artist.

Another village which contests Darley Dale's claim to possession of the oldest Derbyshire yew is Mugginton. Its ancient tree is said to have provided bows for archers who also sharpened their arrows on stones of the church porch, wearing grooves in the masonry. It was believed that this practice would make the arrows more effective in their mission, either in hunting or warfare. Similar grooves are scored in the natural stone of Burycliffe Cave, near Elton, where a rudely incised cross provides evidence that it was the hermitage occupied by some holy man.

Another tree of which I have read was a silver birch which was tapped each year to produce an alcoholic beverage. It grew—and probably still does—in the orchard of the Shoulder of Mutton Hotel at Hardstoft, near Hardwick Hall. The liquid was tapped in spring before the leaves had formed, and yielded six to eight pints each year. Sugar, lemon juice and ginger were added to make a strong intoxicating liquor. The sap of the silver birch was extracted in large quantities in Cornwall where it was shipped in casks to Liverpool. Some trees yielded as much as five gallons a year.

The tiny village of Sheldon was once famous for its Duck Tree. Post-cards showing this phenomenon and giving particulars of its history could formerly be purchased in the nearby village of Ashford-in-the-Water where the "duck boards" used to be on display as a rare curiosity. During the year 1601 a duck was seen to fly over the village green at Sheldon and disappear into the foliage of an ash tree from which it was never observed to reappear. Witnesses concluded that it must have entered a crevice in the tree and, unable to extricate itself, had died. The tree was ever afterwards recognised as the Duck Tree and the legend was kept alive by successive generations calling it by this name. When it became badly decayed at the bole, about the beginning of the present century, it was complained that the tree was a threat to passing vehicles and pedestrians, and the authorities decided to cut it down. The sentence was carried out and the tree removed to a timber-yard at Ashford-in-the-Water where it was sawn into planks; and, right in the core of the tree, engrained in the actual wood, was the impression of the long dead duck. Its measurements corresponded with those of a living bird, and it was concluded that holes pierced through the wood in the area of the brain, lights and liver were caused before, or during, the decay of these organs. After being on display as show-pieces in the village post office, the two boards came into the possession of the then owner of Greatbach Hall who had them

French-polished and incorporated in a mantel-piece of his home.

Not far away from Ashford is Hassop Hall where a beech tree was once credited with the faculty of prophetic speech, although its eloquence was limited to the repetition of a single sentence. Ownership of the Hassop estate was for a long time the subject of controversy, and dramatic stories are told of prolonged legal disputes and pages torn, or entries deleted, from the parish registers of several Derbyshire churches to confuse the claims of the rightful owners. The Hall had its stories of ghosts, too, for I have heard of a lady who, while on a visit to this mansion, left her bedroom during the night with the utmost precipitation to knock up the landlord of the nearby Eyre Arms where she spent the remainder of the night. A piece of red baize from the scaffold of Charles Radcliffe who was beheaded in 1745 was preserved at the Hall for many years.

The story of the Hassop beech is told as follows:- "There is a peculiar story about the old beech that overshadows the ground in front of the old mansion (the residence of the late Earl of Newburgh) at Hassop. It should be mentioned that the ownership of the Hassop estates is still in dispute (at the time of this record), and the story goes that when the wind is exactly in the west, the rustling of the tree in question distinctly murmurs. 'All hail, true heir, that stills my voice! All hail, true heir that stills my voice!' Some say the words are 'All hail the Eyre that stills my voice!' Local tradition has it that many futile attempts have, during the past twenty or thirty years, been made to hew down this strange messenger of nature by current holders of the estate; that no sooner has the axe been taken up than some accident happens to the would-be destroyer, and that within or beneath the tree are buried certain missing documents which will only be discovered by him at whose hand the tree is fated to fall, and who is ignorant of, or neglectful to establish his rights."

The Mandrake Tree, or Haunted Oak, in the grounds of The Hagge, near Staveley, was probably planted during the reign of Henry VIII and flourished until the 19th century, being blown down during a terrible gale on December 12th, 1883.
It had been chained together and buttressed by banks of earth for many years, and was regarded with veneration by the local population. Colonel Colepepper, who married the daughter of Lord de Freschville, wrote concerning the tree:- "I have been at Staveley where my dear wife was born. Near to the Hagge, where she is living, is an Oak Tree which hath mistletoe, the only Oak Tree in England which hath mistletoe at this time." The mistletoe was still flourishing in 1808.

Mr. Godfrey Swift, who lived at The Hagge, wrote:- "You know well how my mother was versed in the folk-lore of the district; when I was quite young she fired my imagination about it with the local stories of how it had been heard to shriek when someone had cut a bough from it at some long past period. It was known also to the wiseacres of the neighbourhood in my grandfather's time as the 'Mandrake Tree', a term fraught to them with terrible mystery. As a boy I made several attempts to see it, but it was closely guarded by an old ogre, the last of the male Froggatts who lived at the Hagge—old Richard Froggatt—and it was not until I was entering upon my teens that I obtained a sight of it. It was then strongly, but rudely fenced round with timber, to prevent the cattle, as I thought, from injuring it". It was later supported by a bank of earth and a wall was built as a further protection.

The Mandrake Tree had its own poet in Mrs. H. Swift who composed a poem a century ago in which the following verses occur:-

When falls eve's gentle twilight
O'er meadow, wood, and lea,
Can you walk with steps unfaltering
Beneath the haunted tree?

Dare you pluck with grasp unsparing
A living branch away;
Nor shriek to see the red drop
Gush from that broken spray?

Yet the hamlets have a legend,
(Uncertain why or how)
A spirit watches o'er the oak
To guard each living bough.

But whether fay or goblin sprite
Thro' powerful word and spell
Dwells there by necromantic art
No chronicles can tell.

Nor when it gained the Eastern name,
That object of affright,
The bloody 'mandrake's' fleshy stem
Which shrieks when torn at night . . .

Time lessens all distinctions;
An innovator came;
Oblivious cloudy mantle
For ever shrouds his name.

He, with the woodman's keen broad axe,
Gave the Oak a sturdy blow
And quickly from the fissure
Fresh crimson drops did flow.

46

Bystanders heard with horror
Fierce words of sudden doom,
Breathing within that ample trunk
Like warning from a tomb.

'Beware! take heed; for it is decreed
When destruction's stroke fells that mighty oak
From balcony to foundation stone
That mansion high shall be overthrown,
And so widely is its desolation spread,
That its ruins shall fall on its master's head.'

Amazement seized all hearers;
They closed the gaping wound,
And round the tree of stones and earth
Raised carefully a mound . . .

7. The Witches of Derbyshire

1607. The witches of Bakewell were executed. Nor is it a wonder that innocence should suffer under that weak and witch-ridden monarch, James the First.

THIS irritatingly bald statement is one of the records of outstanding events in Derby which are preserved in Stephen Glover's unpublished *History of Derbyshire*. He gives no name and no actual date, and we are indebted to William Wood's *Tales and Traditions of the Peak* (1862) and William Andrew's *Bygone Derbyshire* (1892) for supplementing details of the incident. Both tell the following story:

Early in the 17th century a certain Mrs. Stafford kept a milliner's business and boarding-house in Bakewell. She was partnered by another person who is thought to have been her sister. A Scotsman, who had previously lodged with Mrs. Stafford, was arrested in a London warehouse and hauled before a magistrate upon suspicion of intended robbery. His clothing was tattered and torn and he accounted for his dishevelled appearance with a most incredible story. The night previous to his arrest he had been lying in bed at his lodgings in Bakewell when he was roused about 3 a.m. by a brilliant light which invaded his bedroom through crevices in the floor-boards. Prompted by curiosity, he crept out of bed and applied his eye to one of the cracks. In the apartment below he saw Mrs. Stafford and her accomplice who were evidently making ready for a journey. Upon completing their preparations, the Scotsman alleged that Mrs. Stafford uttered an incantation which ran:

"Over thick, over thin,
Now devil to the cellar in London,"

While musing upon the strange circumstance, the Scotsman repeated the words he had overheard, but not exactly as pronounced by Mrs. Stafford. He made the mistake of saying:

"Through thick and through thin,
Now devil to the cellar in London,"

48

upon which utterance he was whisked suddenly away as though by a whirlwind, through (not over) village and town, woodland and meadow, hill and dale, streamlet and river until he found himself breathless and dishevelled sitting in the cellar in which he had been apprehended. To his amazement, Mrs. Stafford and her partner were busily engaged in packing bales of silk and muslin and, although obviously annoyed at his unwelcome and unwanted presence, the former handed him a glass of drugged wine which soon beguiled his senses with an irresistible desire to sleep. The rest of the story was confirmed by the watchman.

The Scotsman volunteered the suggestion that, if further positive proof was needed, a warrant should be issued to search the premises at Bakewell when certain articles of his clothing would be found. These garments he described in detail to the amazed magistrate who was so impressed by the story that he declared it to be a clear case of witchcraft. On his instructions a search was subsequently carried out at Mrs. Stafford's house where the incriminating garments were brought to light, and on this slender evidence the two women are said to have been arrested, charged and condemned to death as witches.

The severity of the sentence is difficult to understand. No capital charge of having willed the death of victims was laid against them and there seems to have been no depositions made accusing them of any acts of spite or malevolence. But there is an explanation to this bizarre story. The Scotsman, when lodging with Mrs. Stafford, had fallen into arrears with his rent and had been given notice to quit. In default of payment, she had withheld some of his clothing and it was the discovery of these garments which the owner had described to the magistrate that provided the evidence of "guilt".

Less than half a century later, far more damaging allegations were brought against an Ilkeston widow, and yet she escaped the gallows. Her name was Anne Wagg and, like the Belvoir witch Joan Flowers and her two daughters, she had a feline accomplice to help achieve her nefarious designs. She was charged with having caused the death of several children and some cattle out of sheer spite. From the charges laid against her we learn that one method of immobilising a witch was to thrust a pair of tongs into the fire and she would be powerless until they were withdrawn. Here are some of the charges with which Widow Anne was confronted:

"The Information of Francis Torratt of Ilkestone in the County of Derby Baker, Taken before Gervase Bennett Esq., one of the Justices of peace for this County June the xviiith 1650, upon his oath. "Concerning Ann Wagg of the same Widdow upon Suspicion of being a Witch or useing enchantmt Wereby she hath done hurt & impayred divers persons with their goods.

Saith she hath beene comonly suspected to bee a Witch & about three yeares agone the said Anne did upon a certain Satterday give forth some speeches against this Infor & his Wife to Elizabeth Parkson this Infor then Servt whoe told this Infor of them & the next Lord's Day as this Inforr his Wife & the said Servt weere going to church the said Anne Wagg stood in the way & frowned upon the said maide butt uttered noe Words & presently the Mayd fell sick & was not able to goe a Stones Cast & the same night this Inforr caused his mayd to lye neere to this Infor and his Wife & about nine of the Clock in the night the Mayd Cryed out Ma⁼ter Mr. but this Infor & his Wife being both awake Could not answer her until Something went of the Maydes bed and then this Infor gott of his bed and the Maid said see you not this Catt, looke where shee goes & this Infor could not stir till the Catt was gone & then this Infor went to the Mayd & then shee cryed out of her throate & there her Winde was stopt. And the Mayd havinge formerly heard that the putting the tongues into the fire the Woman if she was a witch Could not goe. She did put the tongues in the fire & the said Anne did not goe till they were taken forth againe. And lately the Minister Mr. Foxes Wife falling suddainely sicke about five weekes since the said Ann was suspected as this Infor hath heard & the said Mr. G. Fox fetcht her donne & his Wife drew blood on her. Ger. Bennett."

"The Information of Wm Smith of Ilkestone in the County of Derby husbandman Taken before Gervase Bennett Esq one of the Justices of peace for the said County June the Six & twentieth 1650. "This Infor saith that about two Monthes since Ann Wagg Came to John Elliott's to desire Milke & shee not being provided to give her went Away Grumbling & this Infor said Would you had given her some but before the next Morning they found a Calfe of theires dead wch was well overnight."

"The Information of Allice the wife of Wm Day of Ilkeston aforesaid taken the same day concerning the same matter. "Saith that about two or Three yeares since one Elizabeth Webster dyed who tooke upon her death that Anne Wagg had done her hurt & this Infor would have had her the said Webster to have forgiven the said Ann Wagg but she refused & would not."

"The Information of Elizabeth the Wife of George Gothard of Ilkestone aforesaide taken concerning the matter. Saith about fifteen yeares since Ann Wag Came to this Infors house to buy some whea but this Infor told her she had promised it her sister & she answered is not my Money as good as hers & the same night this Infors Child fell suddainely sick & was taken with a Continuall Shakeing & soe continued a week and then recovered & by the fourteene dayes the child was well recovered & then the said Ann Wagg the very same Satterday was fortnight came to buy butter but this Infor not haveing any for her she went away & the very same night the Child fell sick suddainely & dyed before morninge."

"The Information of Ann the wife of Tho: Ancoke taken ye same

50

day concerning the same matter. This Informant saith about tenn dayes since she had a daughter about fifteene yeares of age whoe being sick the said Mayd in her sickness & divers of the neighbours had some feare least Anne Wagge had done her some hurt & caused her to be sent for and they asked forgiveness each of other & soe the Girle dyed & in the time of her sickness the mayd said she was witch-ridden for this she knowes because she could not speake."

"The Information of Allice the wife of Wm Carpenter of Ilkestone aforesaid taken the same day Concerning the same matter upon her oath saith Ann Wagg is of ill repute & that about twelve months since this Informant's child was taken suddainely with a shreeking & continued soe about a weeke & then dyed & she being ill reputed before did then Call her a Witch & was the rather induced to beleeve soe by reason the Child was taken with shreeking & foming att the Mouth wch fitts Continued for the space of foure dayes & then the Child dyed.

Gerr. Bennett."

8.

The Lost Lad and the Three Men

Oft as the shepherds o'er the mountains went,
Each cast a stone to mark the strange event;
Till yonder cairn arose which marks the ground
Where the lost lad beneath the rock was found.
(Richard Furness)

THESE are two different stories from different periods of history, yet they have several points of relationship. They are both stories of moorland tragedy; the names of the victims are unknown, and they are still perpetuated by cairns of stone. Marked on the Ordnance Survey maps not far from the former village of Derwent, we find the name "Lost Lad." A few shreds of the story which gave the mountain summit this name have survived in folk literature, although these are so confused and so much in conflict with each other that it is impossible to discriminate between fact and fiction.

William Wood (*Tales and Traditions of the Peak*) told the story in his usual melodramatic style, and his version appears to have found an echo in that of Seth Evans (*Bradwell: Ancient and Modern*), and other local writers. A footnote to Wood's account acknowledges a variety of traditions as to the origin of this place-name. Writing before 1862, he dates the incident from three to four centuries earlier, and gives the age of the central character as about thirteen. This boy often ventured into the wilds around Derwent in quest of hares, rabbits and other game, and on one such occasion was so intent upon the pursuit of his quarry that he found himself in unfamiliar surroundings and unable to retrace his steps home. After a night spent on the mountain side, he was sustained by plucking and eating a few blackberries, which suggests that the incident happened in autumn, whereas Richard Furness makes winter the setting in his poetical version of the story.

Meanwhile the boy's father and neighbours searched the mountainous district to find some trace of him, only to return at night without any report of success. After several days spent in wandering among the solitudes of moor and mountain without any proper nourishment, it is concluded that the starving and exhausted boy

The Hermit's Cave, Deepdale (chapter 5).

The Sheldon Duck boards (chapter 6).

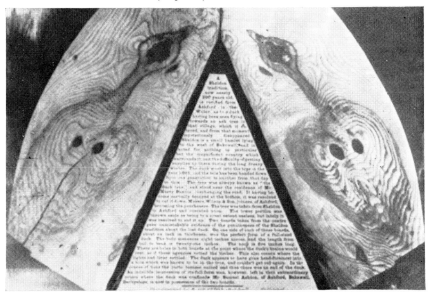

Chatsworth Bridge statue illustrating a story of attempted infanticide. The fallen female statue on the other pier has been replaced with a male figure (chapter 11).

Eagle Stone, Baslow, claimed to be a relic of the pagan god Aigle (chapter 12).

Robin Hood's Stride framed between two of the Grey Ladies where fairies are said to have been seen at their revels (chapters 9 and 13).

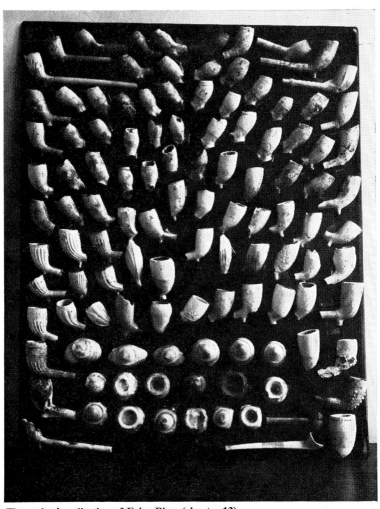

The author's collection of Fairy Pipes (chapter 13).

heaped together a pile of stones, scratching upon them a few particulars of his fate and scrawling in large letters the two words "lost lad." The sorrowing parents mourned their son as dead and it was not until shortly after they themselves had died that sportsmen seeking moorland game found the boy's skeleton lying at the foot of the cairn still bearing its pathetic inscription.

Richard Furness's account of the happening, like that of William Wood, claims a considerable degree of literary licence and occupies the third longest poem in his collected works. Set in the depths of winter, the story gave the poet ample opportunity to use his art of rhetoric in describing the moods of moorland and mountain at this season of the year, and the poem contains some fine descriptive verse. His version also has a happier conclusion than that of Wood.

The poet suggests that the lost lad was a shepherd named Abraham and that his mother was a widow. He went out to round up his flock of sheep on the eve of a threatened snowstorm and, unable to find his way home through the blizzard and darkness, found refuge with his dog in a cave. There he would have perished but for the providential arrival of the local Squire Balguy of Derwent Hall, with his fellow huntsmen and fox-hounds, who accidentally stumbled upon the exhausted pair in their snow-covered retreat. They were restored to home and safety to the great joy of the widow and sympathetic shepherds who had searched the mountains in vain. A foot-note to the poem says:- "This story is founded on fact. To the north of Derwent Hall, the mountain rises to a great height; upon the summit is an immense heap of stones, cast by the shepherds and others upon the Lost Lad's Cave. Few people, who are acquainted with the origin of this cairn, pass by without adding a stone to the existing heap."

The "Three Men" are three cairns which conspicuously prick the skyline on Gardom's Edge east of Baslow. These landmarks have been repeatedly demolished by gamekeepers in past days, only to be re-built by ramblers and local people familiar with their story. The three pyramids of stone recall an incident during the 18th century when three clergymen travelled from Yorkshire to attend the funeral of the Rev. Ralph Rigby who had died after being curate at Eyam for 22 years. He was buried on April 22nd, 1740, in the chancel of Eyam church where a mural pays tribute to his work and worth. After the funeral, the three clergymen set off on foot to make the return journey, but were overtaken by a snowstorm which came on after dark as they travelled over Eastmoor. The men were hopelessly lost in the wilderness of snow and one was found the following morning by a shepherd who managed to restore animation to his frozen limbs. The other two were dead when they were found. Some distance south of this moor is Gladwin's Mark where a man named Gladwin was overtaken by storm and darkness and lost his way. Gathering together a collection of stones he spent the night building and re-building a cairn of stones to keep himself from falling victim to fatigue and exhaustion.

Moss and heather have often provided the couch where lost travellers have slept their final sleep, and Ebenezer Elliott (the Corn Law Rhymer) refers to one of the many such instances which occurred in the Peak District:

> *He died: but still the winds that lov'd him came*
> *And whispered, though he made them no reply;*
> *And still his friends, the clouds, bedew'd his frame*
> *With frozen tears, less cold than charity.*
> *But little men whom summer brought to see*
> *The heathcock's plumes, beheld him where he lay,*
> *And robb'd him of that glorious tomb, which he*
> *Chose in his pride; bearing his bones away*
> *His proud insulted bones—to mix with common clay.*

A remarkable tale is told of a grazier named Barber and his maid-servant who were on a journey to Ireland in 1764 when they were lost on the moors near Hope and their bodies lay covered with snow from January to May. Owing to the stage of decomposition in which the bodies were found, the coroner directed that they should be buried on the spot. Twenty years later, the bodies were exhumed to satisfy the curiosity of some people who were acquainted with the fact that the soil thereabouts had some chemical content which provided a natural process of embalming physical remains. They found the bodies "in no way altered; the colour of the skin being fair and natural, and their flesh as soft as that of persons newly dead. They were exposed for a sight during the twenty years following, though they were much changed in that time, by being uncovered so often. Mr. Henry Brown, M.D., of Chesterfield, saw the man perfect—his beard strong and about a quarter of an inch long: the hair of his head short—his skin hard and tanned a leather colour, pretty much the same as the liquor and earth they lay in. He had on a broad cloth coat, of which the doctor, in vain, tried to tear off a skirt. The woman was more decayed, having been taken out of the ground and rudely handled; her flesh particularly decayed—her hair long and spongy, like that of a living person. Mr. Barber, of Rotherham, the man's grandson, had both bodies exhumed in the presence of the Rev. Mr. Wermald, the then Vicar of Hope, who observed, at their removal, that they lay about a yard deep in moist soil, or moss, but no water stood in the place. He saw their stockings drawn off, and the man's legs, which had been uncovered before, were quite fair—the flesh when pressed pulped a little, and the joints played freely, and without stiffness; the other parts were much decayed. What was left of their clothes, not cut off for curiosity, was firm and good, and the woman had a new serge, which seemed no worse. The bodies were both buried in Hope church, and on some persons looking into their graves some time afterwards, they found them to be entirely decayed."

A similar instance to the above was noted at the neighbouring village of Hathersage when a grave was being prepared in May, 1781, and "the body of Mr. Benjamin Ashton, who was buried on the 29th December, 1725, was taken up, congealed and hard as flint. His breast, belly, and face were nearly the same colour as when he was interred. The coffin was made of oak, one inch and a half thick, and was quite as sound as when first put into the grave, which was so extremely wet that men were employed to ladle out the water, that the coffin might be kept from floating till the body was returned to it. The face was partly decayed, conveying an idea that the putrefactive process had commenced previous to that which hardened the flesh into stone. The head was broken off in removing the body from the coffin, but was placed in its first position when again interred. Mr. Ashton was a corpulent man, who died in the 42nd year of his age."

9.

The Grey Ladies

No, this is not a ghost story. It does not concern the shadowy and insubstantial realms of the supernatural. As a matter of fact it is quite the opposite, for it concerns four solid stone figures which have stood for centuries, losing five of their original number at different periods of time. They are units in what must have been a most impressive circle of nine large stones and were described by Llewellyn Jewitt as being "four old ladies a good deal older than Methuselah." This celebrated antiquary, together with Canon Greenwell, carried out excavations on the site in 1877, but found nothing to throw light on their original purpose. And still they stand, mute and immutable, keeping guard over a secret that science has not been able to discover. The name of the field in which they stand, Nine Stones Close, has outlived the missing stones which have probably been applied to the use of farmers or builders.

Stephen Glover (1829) wrote:- "In a field north of Graned Tor, called Nine Stone Close, are the remains of a Druidical Circle, about thirteen yards in diameter, now consisting of seven rude stones of various dimensions; one of them is about eight feet in height and nine in circumference. Between seventy and eighty yards to the south are two other stones, of similar dimensions, standing erect." This account is confirmed by Thomas Bateman in his *Vestiges of the Antiquities of Derbyshire*.

About 1939, two of the remaining stones had fallen and were re-erected by the efforts of Mr. J. P. Heathcote and his father, the late Mr. J. C. Heathcote, assisted by several interested workers and with the support of the county archaeological society. One of the stones had been leaning dangerously for many years and fell to the ground in 1936, while another was nearly flat. It was thought that it had assumed this semi-recumbent position not long after erection, because of weather grooves worn in its exposed side.

The method of erection by early man is thought to have been by hauling the stones up inclined ramps of earth to then be tilted into the prepared sockets and afterwards packed around the base with earth and stone. The method of re-instating the stone was described by Mr. Heathcote as follows:- "A hole six feet square and three feet deep was dug for the stone. Nothing was found in this soil, although burials and cremation deposits are sometimes found at the foot of the stones. The stone was raised at an angle of 45 degrees by jacks and then pulled into position by pulley blocks. The greatest difficulty was in propping the stone as the work proceeded. The stones were set in concrete beds at exactly the same depth as by the original Bronze Age people about 3,000 years ago." When we think of problems confronting men using modern mechanical methods, we wonder what difficulties the original builders had in handling stones of three tons weight!

The architects and builders of these stone circles provided a puzzle which archaeologists are still seeking to solve. Many theories have been evolved, but none accepted with certainty. It is known how they were built and approximately when, but researchers are still perplexed as to why and for what reason. The Old Testament query is still relevant when it records that "your children shall ask 'What mean ye by these stones?'" It has been speculated that they were centres of pagan sun worship; places of special sanctity memorialising the dead; elaborate sun-dials; signalling stations; primitive theodolites; temples in which Druid priests performed their mystic rites; or sites where fertility cultists practised their magic. Those who could not find a reasoned explanation created legends to account for their existence. Only a few miles away on Stanton Moor the Nine Ladies circle was claimed to be nine maidens dancing on a Sunday to the tune of a fiddler, all of whom were turned into stone as punishment for this act of sacrilege.

But if only these four grey old grannies on Hartle Moor could break their centuries of silence, they would have such a tale to tell the toddlers, for it was in Nine Stones Close that fairies were reputed to have been seen at their revels on moonlight nights. Their nocturnal capers were described most vividly by witnesses who claimed to have watched them dancing to the music of fairy pipers.

The Nine Ladies circle seems to underline the significance of this number in the building of such local landmarks, although here the stones are much smaller in size and embedded in a well defined rampart of earth. This circle is eleven yards in diameter and an isolated boulder known as the King Stone (or Fiddler according to the myth quoted above) may be seen 34 yards away and was undoubtedly connected with the circle. At the Rollright Stones on the Oxfordshire—Warwickshire border, a detached stone is also called the King Stone.

Another landmark of major importance in the county is the Wet Withins circle on Eyam Moor. There are sixteen stones in this circle, similar in size to the ones on Stanton Moor and also projecting from a low mound of earth about 115 ft. in diameter. A large stone, which may have been the capstone of a cist, once occupied the centre. Nearby is a large barrow on the edge of a depression from which the soil composing the mound has evidently been excavated, and also a large cairn of loose stones in which may be seen the remains of a cist. This originally contained a large urn; in it were found calcined bones, ashes, a flint arrow-head, the beak of a large bird and other articles.

A number of circles are known to have been obliterated in the course of agricultural development, but the Ordnance map shows that several may still be located on the moorland heights. It has been suggested that these are in some sort of alignment with each other, and were it not for the gaps caused by those which have disappeared, a pattern could be produced which would help to elucidate the problem as to their original purpose. The most impressive Derbyshire circle is Arbor Low, occupying a prominent position on the heights above Youlgreave, and claiming the distinction of being the third most important circle in the country. With a maximum diameter of 250 ft, it encloses a flat circular area edged by about forty stones lying flat and pointing to the centre. A further assemblage of about thirty weathered limestone monoliths—some 10 or 12 feet long—also lie flat on the ground and it is a matter of conjecture as to whether they ever stood erect. Excavations in 1902 revealed nothing to solve the centuries' old mystery; the most important discoveries consisting of a barbed and tanged arrow-head, a white flint knife, part of a kite-shaped arrow-head and some pieces of Romano-British pottery.

A little distance away, and generally accepted as part of the earthwork complex, is Gib Hill barrow which, it has been noted, bears a similar relationship to the circle as does the King Stone to the Nine Ladies circle. When this barrow was investigated by the Batemans, it was found to contain charcoal, burnt human remains, a flat arrow-head 2 inches long, part of a celt made of basalt, and a small iron fibula with a socket empty of its decorative gem. A neighbouring barrow, smaller in size, contained a female skeleton and that of a child buried in the same cist. In addition to a cow's tooth (perhaps an amulet for they were commonly found in early burials) was a necklace consisting of 416 beads of Kimmeridge coal and a flat pendant of bone ornamented with a pattern of punctures. This was still round the wearer's neck and Bateman described it as "the most elaborate production of the pre-metallic period I have ever seen", and went on to say that "the skull, in perfect preservation, is beautiful in its proportions, and has been selected to appear in the *Crania Britannia* as the type of the British female."

Perhaps this grey lady of the past who thus qualified as a prehistoric pin-up was the wife of a prince or a priest. The elegance of her necklace, and the fact that it probably originated from Dorset, suggests that she was a person of some social status who may have travelled far. Her burial near this ancient cultural centre suggests that she may well have been acquainted with its purpose and with the rites and ceremonies performed within its ambit.

10. An 18th Century Sappho and a 17th Century Sapphira

THIS chapter concerns two ordinary women who are remembered in history for their involvement in extraordinary events. One is a story of pathos and the other a story of perjury.

There are several "lovers' leaps" in Derbyshire. There is one at Matlock, one in Dovedale and another near Buxton, and in Taddington Dale legend tells of the hysterical Hedessa leaping to her death to evade the sensuous clutches of Hulac Warren. The Matlock story seems to have been entirely forgotten, and the one from Buxton is vague and undefined, but the latter differs from most lovers' leap stories in that it concerned two eloping lovers who were being chased by a parental pursuer. The two were mounted on horseback and leaped across the intervening space between the precipices of a narrow limestone gorge. The courage of the father deserted him when he saw the yawning chasm and the gallant lover and his sweetheart made their escape. One is tempted to wonder whether the two were on their way to nearby Peak Forest— the Gretna Green of the Peak— where marriages were solemnised with a minimum of delay.

But the most authentic story is that boasted by Stoney Middleton, for this village remembers the name of the jilted sweetheart who literally leapt to fame when she parachuted into the Dale from a limestone precipice which has ever since been renowned as the "Lover's Leap". The story began to wane when the licence was taken from the inn built at the foot of the precipice. The boldly lettered inscription "Lover's Leap Inn" painted along the facade gradually faded and became obliterated after the building was converted into a transport cafe and unofficial headquarters for the speleologists and climbers who find ample scope for their activities among the caves and crags of Middleton Dale. Horse-drawn brakes used to pull up outside the inn while drivers narrated to the occupants the stirring story of ruined romance which finally prompted Hannah Baddeley to make her leap into the pages of history. In those days the story was an outstanding epic in the history of Stoney Middleton, and visitors gazed with awe at the limestone crags draped with festoons of ivy as they listened to the story of averted tragedy which had been the sensation of the century in that quiet village. Each springtime the grey rocks are splashed with clusters of golden and orange coloured gilliflowers (wall-flowers) which have grown in profusion on the ledges and in the crevices for centuries.

Over two centuries ago, Hannah Baddeley and William Barnsley were the central characters in this drama. Hannah had given William her undivided affection and this had been reciprocated with equal sincerity and singleness of heart. Then something went wrong. The ardour of William began to lose its fire and fervour; the warmth of his kisses were chilled with a feeling of frost until, eventually, he began to avoid her company. A local chronicler wrote: "His visits became less frequent, and soon ceased for ever. But how was this borne by the lovely confiding Hannah? She sank beneath the stroke with all the terrible anguish of a broken spirit. For hours she would sit gazing at the wall in silent stupefaction; then would burst forth a flood of tears, bringing short solace. Like her prototype, sweet Sappho, she often sought her cruel Phaon, but he fled at her approach: thus probing the painful wound his tongue had made. Hapless Hannah! despair at length began to urge her to escape the bitter pangs she endured by self-destruction—awful remedy."

Whether this change in the temperature of William's affection was due to the charms of a rival, we are not told, but Hannah nursed her grief in secrecy for some months. She could find no salve to soothe her wounded spirit; nothing could staunch the bleeding of her heart. Neither the philosophy of friends, nor the counsel of the kind-hearted, could give her the comfort and help she needed to cross her lonely bridge of sighs. She languished like a flower crushed beneath careless feet.

Eventually the girl's position became so intolerable that she decided to make a dramatic exit from the stage of life by flinging herself from the rocks in the Dale. Spurred on by the courage born of despair, she resolutely climbed to one of the steepest points overlooking the village, laid aside her bonnet, scarf and gloves, and made the fateful plunge. Fateful, I repeat, not fatal! For Hannah was wearing a crinoline dress which providentially acted as a parachute, checking her descent. Her fall was further broken by brambles growing upon the ledges of limestone. Like the prodigal son she "came to herself" lying dazed, shaken and bruised in a dry saw-pit near the old carpenter's shop at the foot of the rocks. The course of her descent was marked by fragments of torn garments which fluttered from the bushes above. But Hannah was completely disillusioned as the result of her miraculous escape, and the experience provided a complete cure for her fit of love-sickness.

Hannah survived the experience some years, dying a spinster. Some writers say that she was crippled by her injuries for the rest of her not very long life for in the parish register is the record of her baptism and obituary:- "Hannah, daughter of William and Joan Baddeley, baptised February 22, 1738," and "Hannah Baddeley, buried December 12, 1764." She left a fortune of £180 at her death. The inscription on her tombstone in the churchyard has been deleted by the sandstone surface having peeled away. Although she did not bequeath any charity or dole for annual distribution in the village, she did leave one permanent legacy—the "Lover's Leap." And just recently, the present proprietor of the cafe has revived interest in the story by erecting an impressive sign showing a crinoline-clad maiden tumbling from the limestone precipice above.

The story of Dorothy Matley is epitomised in Ashover parish register where her obituary reads:— "1660. Dorothy Matley, supposed wife of Jno Flint of this parish forswore herselfe; whereupon the ground opened and she sanke over hed Mar. 23rd., and, being found dead, she was buried March 25th."

Somewhere on the disused lead-mine hillocks at Ashover lies buried in a crater of rocks a wooden tub used for "hotching" minerals, a process of separating lead-ore from fluorspar, calcite and other minerals. It was the property of Dorothy Matley, a woman whom no-one appears to have envied and very few admired, a woman whose moral reputation was such that she was branded as "a 17th century Sapphira". Dorothy followed an unusual occupation, for she was employed as a manual worker in the lead-mining industry. Her duties were to wield a flat hammer used in breaking and crushing the mined ore on a "knockstone", and then separating the lead by a crude sieving process. Her story would probably have been forgotten, except that it came to the notice of one of the greatest contemporary writers—John Bunyan.

In his *Life and Death of Mr. Badman*, Bunyan wrote:- "But above all take that dreadful story of Dorothy Matley, an inhabitant of Ashover, in the county of Derby. This Dorothy Matley, saith the relater, was noted by the people of the town to be a great swearer, and curser, and liar, and thief; just like Mr. Badman; and the labour she did usually follow was to wash the rubbish that came forth of the lead mines, and there to get sparks of lead ore. Her usual way of asserting things was with these kinds of imprecations, 'I would that I might sink into the earth if it be not so', or 'I would God make the earth open and swallow me up.' Now upon the 23rd March, 1660, this Dorothy was washing ore upon the top of a steep hill, about a quarter of a mile away from Ashover, and was there taxed by a lad for taking two single pence out of his pocket, for he had laid his breeches by, and was at work in his drawers; but she violently denied it, wishing that the earth might swallow her up if she had them; she also used the same wicked words on several occasions that day.

"Now one George Hodgkinson, an Ashover man of good report

there, came accidentally by where this Dorothy was, and stood awhile to talk with her, as she was washing ore. There stood also a little child by her tub side, and another a distance from her, calling aloud to her to come away; wherefore the said George took the girl by the hand to lead her away to her that called her; but behold they had not gone above ten yards from Dorothy, but they heard her crying out for help, so looking back he saw the woman, her tub and sieve twirling round, and sinking into the ground. Then saith the man, 'Pray God to pardon thy sin, for thou art never like to be seen alive any longer.'

"So she and her tub twirled round and round till they sank three yards into the earth, and there for a while stayed. Then she called again for help, thinking as she said, she would stay there. Now the man, though greatly amazed, did begin to think which way to help her; but immediately a great stone, which had appeared in the earth, fell upon her head and broke her skull, and then the earth broke in on her, and covered her. She was afterwards digged up, and found about four yards within the ground, with the boy's two single pence in her pocket, but her tub and sieve could not be found."

11.

A Short Story

Most people who visit Chatsworth House do so by crossing the ornamental bridge spanning the river Derwent which makes such an attractive foreground feature for many pictures of this famous Derbyshire mansion. This bridge is dubiously claimed to have been designed by Michael Angelo, but a more convincing claim is that the statues adorning the buttresses of its piers represent the work of Caius Gabriel Cibber who carved some of the statuary in the house and its grounds.

On the downstream buttresses of the bridge stand two statues, about which a strange story has been told in former times but has now been almost forgotten. One of the statues is that of a man with a sturdy child poised upon his shoulder as though in the act of flinging it into the water below, while on the opposite buttress is a woman with stone garments streaming in the wind and arms outstretched in a nightmare attempt to save the child. Some years ago, as though it had grown tired of the melodramatic mime, one of the statues plunged into the swirling waters and frogmen had to be engaged to recover the broken pieces.

Many years ago, says the apocryphal story, two servants at Chatsworth formed an attachment which ripened into courtship, but one day, because she could conceal her secret no longer, the girl returned to her home at nearby Bubnell to become an unmarried mother. Shortly after the birth of her baby, the mother was visited in the thatched cottage where she lived by the father of the child. As they talked together in the bedroom to which the mother was still confined, the father suddenly seized the child, dashed downstairs and out of the house towards the river with the frantic, half naked mother in pursuit. Fortunately, the Earl of Devonshire (the incident happened before the Cavendish family had been elevated to ducal status) happened to be passing at the time and he prevented the fellow from carrying out his dastardly intention of drowning the child. A lengthy court case ensued in which the scene of the incident was reported to be one of the artificial lakes adjacent to Chatsworth House and not actually at Bubnell. In the court proceedings the man was favoured by the judge, jury and his titled employer and given quite a lenient sentence.

In his *History of Derbyshire*, Stephen Glover briefly comments on the incident:- "1739. March 22. This evening the assizes ended, before Lord Chief Baron Page, when Mr. James Loton, of Edensor, in the county of Derby, a man of good appearance and considerable substance, was try'd and found guilty of the murder of a male bastard child, by drowning it, and received sentence of death, and to be hanged in chains. It appears from the subsequent papers, that great interest was made on his behalf to save his life. He was respited no less than six times, and finally, in the month of August, received a free pardon when he immediately went home to his family".

Fiction, we see, ever inclined to favour a romantic end to a story, reprieved the child from the fate of being drowned; but fact, always cold and hard, condemned it to that fate. And so, although the incident happened so long ago, the drama is still being enacted on that stone stage beneath the parapet of Chatsworth Bridge, except, as pointed out in the introductory chapter, the story in stone has lost some of its significance by the replacement of the original female figure with that of a male.

12.   Some Superstitions

JUST as "I believe in ghosts" was once a recognised article of the countryman's creed, so his belief in charms, spells, talismans, omens and premonitions kept him in a similar bondage to superstition and fear. Apart from agriculture and the indigenous trades essential to communal life, the oldest industry in Derbyshire is lead-mining and, like sailors, colliers and others who work in hazardous occupations the lives of miners were formerly influenced —if not largely governed—by superstition. Just as they exercised their own peculiar system of autonomy to protect their ancient rights and usages (the Barmote Courts), so they became gradually enslaved to an agglomeration of superstitions which affected their behaviour almost as much as did the lead-mining laws.

At Castleton the miners had a custom of taking a child, with a candle strapped to its forehead, down their mines on the assumption that their speculations would thereafter be assured of success. Whistling was strictly forbidden in the workings, because it was seriously contended that this would drive away the lead-ore. They also believed that lead "grew" in the vein, and this led to the imposition by the clergy of a tithe on the yield of this mineral; a tax which was only commuted after long and expensive litigation when the miners realised the inorganic nature of the mineral. Miners also considered that the appearance of a comet, which they called the Fiery Drake, indicated the existence of a rich vein of ore in the direction to which it pointed. The Knocker, too, was believed to be some supernatural habitue of the mines whose mysterious rappings on the limestone would lead prospectors to the discovery of ore. The knockings have been attributed to dripping water, but this explanation has been confuted by the fact that the knockings are irregular and have a hollow sound.

Referring to a steam pumping-engine used to de-water the workings of Calver Mill Sough which closed in 1794 because of hydrology problems, Miss Nellie Kirkham says:- "It is a local tradition that when this engine did not work the men put bits of wicken (twigs of the rowan tree) on it, as they said it was bewitched. The belief that the rowan tree was a protection against witches and the evil eye goes back to the days of the Norsemen." This same tree was esteemed of great value in preventing witchcraft, and tiny crosses made from its twigs were worn to resist the influences of witches. When butter would not "come", milk-maids placed a rowan twig across the butter-tub to achieve the desired effect. Sometimes the pails (kits) and churns used in dairies were made from rowan wood as a further precaution against witchcraft.

Love charms were a once popular, though not always efficacious, means of inducing the affections of reluctant lovers. One used by a Derbyshire girl named Susan Lebway was contained in a bag folded into small size and enclosing a very small silk sachet which included parings of the finger and toe nails of the love-sick damsel for whose special relief it had been composed. The bag also contained a tiny piece of linen which had been cut or torn off one of her under garments. These items were carefully folded up in the formula, wrapped in two or three thicknesses of linen, tightly stitched up in silk and then worn under the left armpit attached to the inner side of the sleeve of Susan's under-garment. In the left hand upper corner of the formula was the magic square, a block of figures in which the lines when added in every direction arrive at the same total. There were also symbols of the sun and other magical signs, together with the lines:

Susan Lebway to Draw the
Affections of Theobald Young
to herself, So that he Shall
Never have any Rest or Peace
untill he Do Return unto her
And Make her his Lawful Wife
Let the Spirits of the Planets Continually
Torment him untill he do fulfill this
My Request. Cossiel Nachiel Gabriel
I Continualy stir up his Mind thereto.
Fiat Fiat Fiat Cito Cito Cito Amen.

Whether Susan's charm achieved the desired effect on Theobald is not known, but Llewellyn Jewitt, into whose possession it came, reported that the sachet showed evidence of considerable wear.

During the early 17th century, the Rev. John Rowlandson, Vicar of Bakewell, testified against a Glossop webster (weaver) named Hall who had received £3 from the husband of Ellen Gregory of Over Haddon, with the promise of a further £3 for the provision of a charm to cure her of lunacy. Mrs. Gregory seemed to be troubled "with a thinge that was sowed up in a cloth & hunge in a stringe about her neck wch beinge opened, there was founde in it a paper in wch (to my best remembrance) there were about tenn lynes written, but soe as that I could not read all. The wrightinge (as I conceaved) was intended for a charme, or some such like

70

thinge; & (as the poore woman confessed to mee) it was hunge about her necke by one Mr. Hall who had 3 li of her husband in hand, & was to have 3 li more when shee was cured of her lunacy, But yt charme being taken away, the same man comeing to her afterwards did fasten upon her another paper, in which there was nothing soe wrighting as in the former, for uppon ye sight of it I read it & founde that to bee but a peece of the Lord's prayer; I am enformed that this Mr. Hall dwells about Glossop and is by trade a Webster . . ."

John Flamsteed, the first Astronomer Royal, was a native of Derbyshire and he had a rather discomfiting experience when trying to confound the superstitions of his laundress who had somewhat nettled him by her lack of discrimination between the science of astronomy and that of astrology. She had lost her washing and came to the learned doctor with a plea that he would consult the stars as a means of recovering the mislaid or stolen clothes. Deciding to teach her a lesson that would effectively shatter her belief in the influence of the stars on human life, for she refused to be persuaded of the folly and futility of her request, Dr. Flamsteed drew a series of impressive but imaginary diagrams and symbols, and then instructed the expectant watcher that she must go to the middle of a certain field where she *might* find her lost washing. Convinced that the woman would be disillusioned by the apparent miscarriage of his experiment, the astronomer was amazed when she returned to pour out her gratitude for his help, having found the lost washing at the exact spot he had indicated!

Harold Armitage, in his *Chantreyland*, mentions among other superstitions which formerly prevailed in the district, the custom of watching the church to glimpse the funerals of people destined to die the ensuing year. "No farther away than Dronfield an old man used to sit in the porch on the eve of Saint Mark at midnight to watch the spirits of those who would die that year pass into the church, and on the eve of another saint an old woman of Troway told Mr. Addy that it was the custom of girls who wanted to see their future husbands to hang a wet smock or chemise before the fire, and to put a loaf of bread and a knife upon the table. If the apparition of the man who appears turns the smock towards the girl he will marry her. If he cuts a piece from the loaf of bread and eats it he will be a good husband; if he cuts the smock in two a bad one . . ."

James Montgomery, the hymn-writer and former editor of *The Sheffield Iris*, wrote a lengthy poem based on the custom of watching the church porch on St. Mark's Eve. In his *Popular Antiquities*, John Brand wrote that "the third year (for this must be done thrice) the watchers are supposed to see the ghosts of all those who are to die the next year, pass by into the church, (which they are said to do in their usual dress, and precisely in the order of time in

71

which they are doomed to depart. Infants and young children, not yet able to walk, are said to roll in on the pavement. Those who are to die remain in church, but those who are to recover, return after a longer or shorter time, in proportion to the continuance of their future sickness). When anyone sickens that is thought to have been seen in this manner, it is presently whispered about that he will not recover, for that such a one, who has watched St. Mark's Eve, says so. This superstition is in such force, that, if the patients themselves hear of it, they actually despair of recovery . . ." I remember reading of one person whose curiosity in this matter was rewarded by a preview of her own funeral!

William Cundy was a Baslow resident who cultivated this habit of sitting in the porch of the village church every All Hallow's Eve for the same purpose. Whether he was successful in his vigils we do not know, but he was a man to whom mothers regularly resorted with ailing children and farmers with sick cattle, for they all had faith in his knowledge of herbal and other remedies. He also administered love philtres to love-sick men and maidens. The possession of a telescope is said to have assisted him in his study of astronomy and the mysteries of astrology. On one occasion a child was reported missing to old William. The parents and friends had searched frantically everywhere and appealed in desperation for his help. After making mysterious mathematical calculations, he told the searchers that they would find the child asleep within the shadow of the Eagle Stone, a huge mass of rock on the moors nearby, adding that her bonnet would be found lying at her side. The father hastened to the place and found his little daughter sound asleep and, sure enough, lying by her side was the child's bonnet.

The Eagle Stone is an island of gritstone rock from which the surrounding strata has been worn away by centuries of erosion. Far across the valley, on another escarpment where stands the Nelson Monument, are three crags resembling—with the exercise of some imagination—the hulls of galleons. They have been respectively inscribed "Victory", "Royal Soverin" and "Defiance". Eagle Stone is said to be a corruption of Aigle's Stone, one of the huge missiles flung by the pagan god, Aigle, who was reputed to be so powerful that he could toss with ease objects which humans were unable to lift. Dr. Addey, however, says that the name derives from Egglestone, or Witch Stone, and that Baslow girls would not accept the advances of any male unless he had proved his manhood by scaling the rock and thus won favour with the witches. The rock is scratched and scored by countless clambering feet, but nowadays the achievement is only attempted by climbers practising their skill and prowess in this ever popular sport.

Another legendary figure was Hob whose name survives in several place-names, some of which are attached to prehistoric

Monsal Dale from the castellated rocks of Hob's Hurst House.

tumuli. Not far from Buxton there is a Hob's Hurst House which consists of a cave where a large number of Romano-British objects —including coins, ceramics, ornaments and even coal—have been found buried beneath a layer of stalagmite five feet thick in places. Near this cave is a spring, the waters of which have been so charmed by the mysterious Hob that all who drink there on Good Friday, with faith in its healing virtues, will be healed of their complaints. This seems a rather strange blend of pagan and Christian tradition.

Referring to Hob's House in Monsal Dale, Ebenezer Rhodes (*Peak Scenery*) wrote:- "On the steep side of Great Finn, an insulated rock that is split and rent into parts like the ruins of a castle rises from out the thick underwood with which the hill is covered: this shapeless mass is called Hob's House, and tradition states that it was inhabited by a being of gigantic stature, who was possessed of great and mysterious powers, and who was known by the name of Hob. This extraordinary personage never appeared by day; but when the inhabitants were asleep in their beds, he traversed the vales, entered their houses, thrashed their corn, and in one single night did the work of ten day labourers, unseen and unheard, for which service he was recompensed with a bowl of cream, that was duly placed upon the hearth, to be quaffed on the completion of the task he had voluntarily imposed upon himself." Milton describes the legend in his *L'Allegro*.

Apart from their long recognised value as medicines, magical properties were ascribed to certain herbs and plants. The seeds of fern, for example, were supposed to make invisible those who had a certain formula in their possession; they could also raise the spirits of departed friends, and had the mystic power of bringing future lovers into the presence of their mistresses. A certain ritual attended the collection of these dangerous and dynamic seeds which, to prove effective, had to be gathered on St. John the Baptist's Eve. Ben Jonson makes the following allusion to the belief in invisibility:-

I had
No medicine, Sir, to go invisible,
No fern-seed in my pocket.

Llewellyn Jewitt, the Derbyshire antiquary, referred to this custom as follows:- "In many parts of the country it is still usual for the rustic maidens and youths, too, to gather the fern-seed, and for this purpose much caution is used. The person intending to gather it fasts during the evening, and then shortly before midnight proceeds carefully and noiselessly to the plant, kneels down before it, and places a vessel on paper beneath its leaves and waits patiently for the seed to discharge itself and fall into the receptacle which is held, of its own accord, and without shaking the plant, except it be with a hazel wand. This is then most carefully preserved and carried home for use. Arrived at home the doors are opened, not a word is spoken, the table is silently laid with bread and cheese and best beer, and some of the fern is sprinkled on the cloth. The expectant maidens then sit down as if to eat, but not a morsel is touched, or word spoken, and after a time the young men whom they are destined to marry are supposed to enter the room, walk up to the table, and bowing lovingly each to his intended, take up a glass and noiselessly drink, and they pass out by the opposite door as noiselessly as they entered. The charm thus being broken, the young women empty the glasses out of which their lovers had in spirit sipped, and then retire to rest, placing the fern seed under their pillow to dream on.

"In some parts of the Peak a somewhat different custom formerly prevailed. The fern seed having been procured, was placed, with a pen-knife, on a clean cloth in the centre of the room, the maidens then hung a clean undergarment on a chair before the fire, and waited the denouement in silence. If the young woman was destined to be married 'before the year was out', her lover was supposed to enter by the open door, take up the knife, cut a hole in the garment, and pass out again . . ." A sprig of sage immersed in a bowl of rose water was supposed to possess similar virtue.

Ferns had another strange use in former times for, during periods of excessively dry weather, it was the custom to use them for bonfire fuel with the object of inducing, or producing, rain. After staying at Bolsover Castle during the summer of 1636, Charles I wished to be assured of fine weather while in the area and had a letter written to the High Sheriff of Stafford prohibiting such bonfires:- "His Majesty taking notice of an opinion entertained in Staffordshire, that the burning of ferne doth draw rain down, and being desirous that the country and himself may enjoy fair weather as long as he remains in these parts, his Majesty hath commanded me to write unto you to cause all burning of ferne to be forborne until his Majesty has passed the country . . ."

Hemp seed was another means of producing a materialisation of future husbands and a writer tells of the prevalence of this custom at Ashbourne:- "Among the many curious relics of superstition remaining in this locality is the following, which we have known practised within a few years—If a young woman wishes to divine who is to be her future husband, she goes into the churchyard at midnight, and, as the clock strikes twelve, commences running round the church, repeating without intermission:

I sow hemp seed, hemp seed I sow,
  He that loves me best,
Come after me and mow.

And having performed the circuit of the church twelve times without stopping, the figure of her lover is supposed to appear and follow her. It is not so many years since a young woman, having been persuaded to try this charm, was so overcome with the excitement, fear, and fatigue, perhaps from the exertion, that when she had completed her task she fainted and fell, was carried home, and soon afterwards died."

I was told of a farmer's wife who, possessing the gift of divination, was asked by her maid if she could name her future husband. The girl was advised to sow hemp seed round the well at midnight, whereupon her husband-to-be would be revealed to her in person. Next morning the mistress enquired, "Well, did you see your future husband last night?"

To which the maid replied in a tone which implied that she had had but little faith in the experiment: "Nay, Ah only seed t' mester wi' a scythe ower his showder." Nor could she understand why her mistress suddenly turned pale and faint. But, shortly afterwards, the farmer's wife died and the maid was invited to fill the vacancy—and accepted!

Mrs. Johnson at Youlgreave possessed this uncanny gift as the result of being a twin born at midnight. Asked by a local youth whether she could enlighten him as to the name of the girl he would marry, she replied, "I can't tell you her name, but I can tell you her initials." Taking a large old-fashioned iron key, she placed the loop on the young man's forefinger and asked her son to grip tightly the part that fits into the lock. She next supplied the youth with a copy of the Bible and asked him to read a certain passage of Scripture, following which he must slowly repeat the letters of the alphabet. Upon reaching the letter "e", the key was snatched from the grasp of the holder and began to revolve round the young man's finger at a rapid speed. A further trial resulted in a repetition of the happening, and at a later letter the same thing occurred. Years afterwards the subject of the experiment—who had gone to live at Sheffield and in the meantime had got married—returned to Youlgreave to renew acquaintance with the Johnson family. During the conversation he was asked by Mrs. Johnson the maiden name of his wife and, although he had forgotten the incident, his reply proved the accuracy of the forecast of the twin born at midnight.

A most satisfactory love philtre was formerly produced by toadstools gathered at the full moon, carried home without being touched or breathed upon, and then placed with a live toad into a clean, new earthen pipkin containing fresh spring water and set to seethe in the oven. When perfectly cooked, the maiden desiring to compel the presence of her lover had to drink five drops of liquor and repeat a certain magic formula. Toadstools were also regarded as an infallible remedy for epilepsy. They had to be gathered just as they were forcing their way through the earth and swallowed in claret at midnight.

So, whatever the malady—love-sickness, lunacy or epilepsy, the desire to discover mineral wealth or the identity of a future partner —the people of Derbyshire found remedies supplied by plants and planets, charms and charlatans, philtres and fungus, or the skill of those who had inherited the key to unlock the mysteries and secrets of the future.

13.   A Chapter for Children

Just as "I believe in phantoms" was a firmly held article in the countryman's creed, so there used to be a widespread belief in the existence of fairies. Such relics as the tiny bowls of clay pipes and arrow-heads of prehistoric man were dug up in gardens or ploughed to the surface in fields, and these were called "fairy pipes" and "elfin darts", the latter sometimes being mounted in silver and worn as charms. In the meadows the darker green grasses of fungi rings, where mushrooms and toadstools flourish in their season, were believed to be the "fairy rings" where the little folk held their moonlight revels.

The circle has always been a figure of mystical significance and even the prehistoric stone circles—claimed as centres of Druid ritual and worship —where thought to have some connection with the fairy kingdom. The Nine Ladies Circle on Stanton Moor is a typical example, although tradition argues that these are maidens turned into stone for dancing on a Sunday to the tune of "the fiddler standing by" who is also petrified for encouraging this act of sacrilege. Mary Howitt, the Derbyshire poetess, wrote a charming poem entitled "The Fairies of Caldon Low" concerning another prehistoric site which rural tradition claimed was populated at certain times by the little people, and this poem was alway a part of the literary curriculum of Derbyshire schools a generation ago.

About two miles west of the Stanton circle is Nine Ladies Close where only four of the original nine monoliths remain standing. Llewellyn Jewitt, founder and editor of *The Reliquary*, lived at nearby Winster Hall and heard the following stories concerning fairies: "Of the Hartle Moor circle only four stones now remain. Around this Druidical circle it is said—and believed in by some of the people of the district—the fairies meet on certain occasions—the full moon, I believe, at midnight, and dance and hold 'high jubilee'. So firmly is this believed that I have been told with extreme seriousness of people who, passing at that time of night, have not only seen the dance but heard the 'fairy pipes' of another kind than those I am about to allude to—the musical instruments—playing for them to dance to. I have heard it seriously affirmed that there were 'hundreds of fairies', gentlemen and ladies, some dancing, others sitting on the stones or the grass around and others playing the music; while others, again, strolled about in loving couples among the fern and bracken. Well, one day a farm labourer turned up a pipe—a 'fairy pipe' of the kind I am about to speak of—and, being pretty nearly his dinner time, he sat down on the soft turf at the foot of a mass of fallen rock, and taking out his knife, began cleaning out the soil from the bowl. Having done this and made it usable, he filled it with tobacco and began to smoke.

"The taste of the tobacco seemed to him to be peculiarly sweet and delicious and the scent more fragrant than any he had experienced from any other pipe. He was so delighted with it and the bowl being very small and soon emptied, that he refilled it and again began puffing away in perfect enjoyment. He had only taken two or three puffs at the second filling however, when he began to feel his eyes 'go queer' . . . At last he thought he was turning blind; a film came over his eyes and he could scarcely see even the mid-day sun. All at once the film began to pass away, like a mist rising from a valley, and instead of his ordinary vision, he had the power of seeing what no mortal before had ever seen.

"In front of him, beneath a large stone, he saw, as it were, the ground transparent, and far below, deep down beneath the surface, was another world, more beautiful than anything he had ever dreamed of—rocks, and trees, and streams, and flowers, and palaces, and beautiful birds were not a tithe of what he saw; and more wonderful still, there were hundreds upon hundreds of 'small people' gaily dressed, and enjoying and disporting themselves in every imaginable way. It was perfectly fairyland. How long he sat there watching these little folks and admiring their subterranean world of beauties, he did not know; but at length the film came back gradually upon his eyes, the smarting returned, the vision passed away, and, his pipe gone out, he was once more able to see as of old.

"Each time he smoked the pipe after that, the same sensations came over him and the same scene became visible to his eyes; so he knew it was the effects of smoking an elfin-pipe. The Fairy Pipes' which I have named are the bowls of the very old pipes, many of them dating back a couple of centuries, that are not unfrequently dug up in gardens or unearthed by the plough. They are of course of small size in comparison with those now in use and are in Derbyshire and elsewhere popularly known as Fairy Pipes, Elfin Pipes, Mab Pipes and the like . . ."

Clay pipes are occasionally found in old lead-mine workings, as well as in gardens and ploughed fields, and Jewitt goes on to tell the following story:- "A lead miner who was busying himself in the old workings of a mine— 'Carl's Work' or 'Old Man's Work' as these old workings are called—on Brassington Moor, found one of these veritable little 'fairy pipes' and put it into his waist-coat pocket, intending to bring it to me, knowing that I am interested in all these matters and glad to add anything curious to my collection. He had not had it there long when he felt, he said, 'pricks all o'er him o' that side'. Not knowing how to account for it, he took out all the things from his pocket—among the rest this pipe and tobacco box—thinking there might be something there that pricked him. Finding nothing he this time put the pipe in the pocket on the other side, when immediately he felt the same irritating feeling there, and again changed their position—this time, and with like result, to his trousers pocket. He then began to think it must in some way—but how he could not tell—be the pipe that produced this effect; so he put it into his jacket pocket and thought no more about it for an hour or so. When he put his jacket on he found the pocket smouldering, for the pipe had burnt its way through and was 'clean gone!' although he had no matches about him nor had smoked the whole of that day. The pipe was never more seen and consequently was not added to my collection. Its loss was, however, amply compensated for by the telling of his story; and when I said, 'but how could the pipe prick you or burn your pocket, or get itself away from you?' by his look as he replied: 'Sir, it worn't the pipe as done it; it wur th' elves as took it off'.

"In another Peak locality a labouring man, after his day's work, was digging in his own cottage garden one evening when, as luck would have it, he turned up a 'fairy pipe'. Unlike most that are found, this one had a short piece of stem still attached to the bowl. On stooping down to pick it up, thinking to turn his find to good account for smoking, the man was no little surprised and startled to see one of the 'little people'—an old wizened man dressed in green—sitting astride of the stem, and who, with his arms akimbo, looked up at him with a droll but not very pleasant expression on his face. The labourer looked hard at the little fellow, scarcely believing his senses, and stooped a little closer, the better to examine him, and to make out what he could be. On this, the sprite—for it was no other—who had hitherto been eyeing him attentively, sprang to his feet, stood on the bowl of the pipe, and putting himself in a defiant attitude, assumed such a diabolical look that he drew back in fright, and let his spade fall. On again turning his head, both pipe and sprite were gone, and all his digging and searching were vain; they were never again seen.

"In another instance, in pretty nearly the same locality, the picking up of a 'fairy pipe' had a remarkable effect on its finder. In that instance the man, a lead miner, picked up the pipe and, as in the case of the last anecdote I have related, it had a piece of the stem still attached to the bowl and was therefore adapted for smoking. Having filled it the man, so the story was told to me, took a whiff or two, much to his satisfaction. Just when the smoke began gracefully to curl about him, he saw the air, wherever a curl of the smoke made its way, filled with fairies, each of which was furnished with butterfly wings. These flew and wheeled round him by scores; and while some lit on his nose, his eyes and his ears, and bit and pinched and scratched him, others in myriads stuck little darts like those of raspberry bushes, into his skin till he could not bear. At length taking his pipe from his mouth, he swore, and threw it down on the ground, when it was instantly caught up by the host of flying fairies and carried off, no one knew whither, and he saw it no more. 'And a good riddance to it,' the man said emphatically."